101 ESSENTIAL LISTS
FOR SENCOS

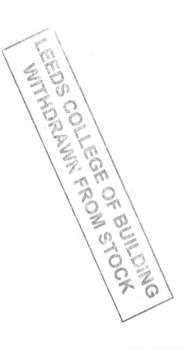

101 ESSENTIAL LISTS SERIES

101 ESSENTIAL LISTS
FOR SENCOS

Kate Griffiths and Jo Haines

continuum
LONDON • NEW YORK

Continuum International Publishing Group
The Tower Building   80 Maiden Lane
11 York Road   Suite 704
London   New York
SE1 7NX   NY 10038

www.continuumbooks.com

© Kate Griffiths and Jo Haines 2006

British Library Cataloguing-in-Publication Data
A catalogue record for this book is available from the British Library.

ISBN: 0-8264-8865-X (paperback)

Library of Congress Cataloging-in-Publication Data
A catalog record for this book is available from the Library of Congress.

Typeset by YHT Ltd
Printed and bound in Great Britain by Ashford Colour Press Ltd,
Gosport, Hants

CONTENTS

The Role of the SENCO

1

 The job description

The role of the Special Educational Needs Coordinator, (SENCO) can differ widely, depending on the age of the children and the type of school in which you work. However, there are some general responsibilities that apply from early years through to secondary.

Teaching, learning and assessment for pupils with SEN

- ○ Identify and adopt the most effective teaching methods.
- ○ Monitor teaching and learning.
- ○ Identify and teach skills that will develop pupils' ability to work independently.
- ○ Set targets for raising achievement.
- ○ Collect and interpret specialist assessment information.
- ○ Set up systems for identifying, assessing and reviewing pupils.
- ○ Keep the headteacher and governing body up to date on the effectiveness of SEN provision.
- ○ Develop understanding of learning needs and the importance of raising achievement among pupils.
- ○ Liaise with staff to ensure that pupils transfer smoothly from class to class and school to school.
- ○ Keep parents informed about their children's progress.

Leadership

- ○ Encourage all members of staff to recognize and fulfil their responsibilities to pupils with SEN.
- ○ Provide training opportunities for teaching assistants and other teachers to learn about SEN.
- ○ Spread good practice in SEN across the school.
- ○ Identify resources needed to meet the needs of pupils with SEN and advise the headteacher of the necessary costs.

The multi-talented SENCO

A good SENCO requires a variety of different skills and qualities. You need to be able to multi-task and to be multi-talented! Apart from diplomacy and boundless patience, the following qualities are prerequisites for the job.

Leader:

- ability to motivate and inspire others
- ability to analyse yourself
- ability to challenge.

Teacher of:

- the curriculum
- basic skills
- organizational skills
- social and life skills
- behaviour management.

Assessor of:

- pupil progress in the curriculum
- progress in life and social skills
- the need for access arrangements
- the general effectiveness of SEN provision.

Adviser on:

- facilitating access
- meeting the needs of SEN pupils in mainstream settings
- SEN in all curriculum areas.

Interpreter of:

- legislation
- subject information
- guidance from DfES and other organizations.

Reviewer of:

- pupil progress
- the effectiveness and impact on school of SEN policy
- staff effectiveness
- the use of resources.

LIST 3

Other talents required

In addition to some of the more obvious qualities that you need for the job, you'll also find you need skills in other areas.

Budgetary controller:

○ knowledge of funds for SEN within school
○ management of SEN budget in consultation with the headteacher and financial manager
○ bidder for new funds.

Human resource manager:

○ recruiter of staff
○ developer of job descriptions and staff skills
○ interviewer
○ negotiator
○ peacemaker
○ diplomat.

Strategist:

○ establisher of mission and aims
○ writer and reviewer of the SEN policy and development plan
○ leader of working groups
○ writer and reviewer of curriculum guidelines
○ analyser and collator of data.

Liaiser and negotiator with:

○ the senior management team
○ neighbouring schools and local special schools
○ governors
○ parents
○ other agencies
○ other curriculum leaders, heads of years and form and class teachers
○ subject and SEN associations.

Time manager:

○ ability to prioritize
○ ability to find 25 hours in a day!

Writer of:

- IEPs, management profiles and reviews
- provision maps
- policies
- advice for staff
- advice for formal assessment
- reports for governors
- information for tribunals.

Advocate for:

- SEN
- pupils
- support staff
- parents.

And!

- patience of Job
- ability to work 24/7
- miracle worker!

LIST 4 A prayer

A daily recitation of the prayer below might be necessary!

Dear God

So far today I've done all right.
I haven't gossiped,
I haven't lost my temper,
I haven't criticized or moaned.

I haven't been snappy, grumpy, nasty, selfish or over indulgent.
I'm very thankful for that.

But in a few minutes, Lord,
I'm going to get out of bed,
And from then on,
I'm probably going to need a lot more help.

Amen

Getting Organized 2

Are you a good time manager?

There are many demands on a SENCO's time so it is important that you manage your time well. Use these questions to work out where you might be going wrong.

- What is my biggest problem?
- On what or on whom am I spending too much time?
- Do I need to attend all the meetings?
- Do I know the time of day when I am most effective?
- Can I delegate any of my work?
- How much of my time is planned? Can I change this?
- How many interruptions are there in my day?
- Do I organize my day?
- Have I learnt to say 'no'?
- Can I cut down on travelling time, e.g. by avoiding busy times?

Time-management tips

It is possible to improve your time-management skills. Here are some tips to help you to be more effective.

○ Have a fixed routine. Give yourself set times in the day to do paperwork such as individual education plans (IEPs), reviews and timetables. Make yourself unavailable at these times.
○ Do the most important things at the time of day you work most efficiently.
○ Set deadlines for your jobs and stick to them.
○ Do not put off the difficult jobs because you don't want to do them. They are not going to become any easier by delaying the start.
○ Check how often and why you are interrupted and see if you can lessen these moments.
○ Tell your colleagues or a teaching assistant (TA) when you do not want to be interrupted and let them know the times when you will be available.
○ Don't try to do more than one thing at a time, but do keep a list of the other things that need finishing.
○ When you are going to make a phone call, decide in advance what you want to find out or what you want to say.
○ Jot down ideas as you think of them – post-it notes are very good for this.
○ Try to finish work you have started. If you keep going back to it, the work could become disjointed and you could lose your train of thought.
○ Agree specific times when you will discuss things with TAs and other teachers. You could have a 'surgery' to discuss issues. A weekly meeting with TAs can be a useful time to share information.
○ At the end of the week, review how you have used your time and work out if you could have used it more efficiently.
○ Don't take work home unless you really are going to work on it. Try to finish the paperwork at school and leave home for leisure.
○ Be assertive and don't be afraid to say 'no'.

Chairing meetings

As a SENCO you may frequently be asked to chair meetings. With the Every Child Matters agenda (see List 70 Every Child Matters) you could even find yourself chairing large multi-agency groups. Being a good chair is very important for a successful outcome of a meeting.

A good chair will:

○ state the purpose and objectives of the meeting and have an agenda ready

○ make sure that someone is available to take accurate minutes

○ make sure that everyone is introduced and that their role is clarified

○ start and finish on time

○ manage the discussions and make sure that they further the aims of the meeting

○ ensure that only one person is speaking at a time and that everyone has an opportunity to contribute and participate

○ manage any difficult situations, remaining calm and in control of the meeting

○ follow the agenda and allocate time according to the importance of the agenda item

○ keep participants to the point

○ summarize agreements, actions and accountabilities and make sure that these are clearly flagged up in the minutes

○ check the action noted in the minutes is taken.

Writing reports

LIST 8

SENCOs are often expected to write reports. These may be for:

o an annual review of a pupil with a statement
o formal assessment
o governors (the annual report)
o parents and school staff (on the outcome of assessment)
o SEN tribunals
o school (evaluation reports on SEN provision)
o multi-agency meetings.

It is important that you become a competent report writer. Here are some top tips.

o Be focused – what is the report to be about?
o Know your target audience – who wants the report and why? What will happen as a result of the report? What are they going to do with the information they are looking for?
o Consider the scope of the report – what should it contain? What should it not contain?
o Decide the size of the report – how long should it be? What is expected? Very often you will find a list of items that need addressing. The SEN Code of Practice and the Toolkit give some help here (see List 62 SEN Code of Practice).
o Know what you want to say – what messages are you trying to get over?
o Outline your report – if an outline of what is needed is not available, think of the areas that you need to cover and make a list of them.
o Gather and collate information – details about pupils should be collected from all those involved with the child. Make sure you have included parents' views and also sought the views of the pupil. For other reports, ask those who hold the relevant information. Stick to facts, be objective and avoid opinion as far as possible.
o Avoid jargon – read through your report to check that you have explained any specific terms. Check that it can be easily understood by the intended audience.
o Check the report – does it meet the objectives? Are the key messages clear and supported by the content of the report? Proofread it carefully.

LIST 9 Timetables

It is very often the SENCO's job to organize the timetables for support staff. In a large secondary school this could involve doing the timetables for over 20 people and it is important to be well organized and clear about the priorities.

○ Link the timetable to the needs of the pupils (provision maps can be useful here, see List 66 Provision maps).

○ Make sure you have addressed all the provision required on a pupil's statement.

○ Make sure that the adult is supporting in the classroom for a specific purpose, e.g. to deliver a small-group literacy programme, to run a programme to raise the self-esteem of pupils, to support poorly coordinated pupils in a practical subject or to help a pupil with autistic spectrum disorder cope with a challenging situation.

○ In a secondary school, consider timetabling teaching assistants to a particular faculty. This not only makes planning and evaluation time easier to arrange but it also means that the teaching assistant develops subject expertise and can offer more effective support to pupils.

○ If you decide not to put the teaching assistants in faculties, try to make sure that the same person supports the same group for one subject, e.g. make sure that all the Year 7 English lessons for a particular group are supported by the same person.

○ Ensure that the support is available for the optimum amount of time. It is not useful to put an hour's support in for a particular programme which only lasts 20 minutes. Vary your support to fit in with the concentration span of the pupil. Individual and small-group support is very intensive for a pupil who may not be able to sustain long periods of attention.

○ Don't set your timetable in tablets of stone at the beginning of the year. Constantly revisit it and make sure that you are making the best use of a very valuable resource. Use a system for recording the timetable that can be easily changed so that you are not constantly rewriting it. There are commercial systems on the market that may be useful.

○ If possible, make time to observe the use of support in a classroom or ask the teacher to evaluate the efficacy of the support after a few weeks.
○ Make time to discuss the timetables with support staff. They often have excellent suggestions for making support more effective.

LIST 10

Effective planning, monitoring and evaluation

As a SENCO it is very important to monitor and evaluate provision, progress and plans on a regular basis. The following framework may be helpful:

○ Draw up a strategic development plan of policy and provision in partnership with the headteacher, governors and/or other appropriate colleagues. Review it annually.

○ Monitor SEN policy and practice for effectiveness and review them annually to check that they include any new guidelines or practices. (The 17 points listed on page 197 of the SEN Code of Practice give the information that should be included in an SEN/inclusion policy.)

○ Check with the headteacher that there is an accessibility plan in place and that it includes plans to make adaptations to the curriculum as well as the physical environment.

○ Seek and take into account pupils' views.

○ Seek and take into account parents' views.

○ Put in place an ongoing and systematic framework for the self-review of SEN provision in school, including its effectiveness and impact, involving monitoring and evaluation.

○ Track the progress of pupils.

○ Monitor the effectiveness of targets.

Getting on top of administration

You will make your life a lot easier if you can be organized and get all those administrative jobs under control. So:

○ Review pupil records at least twice yearly and maintain them in accordance with recommendations in the Code of Practice.
○ Make all staff aware of relevant proformas and know how to complete and use them.
○ Use ICT and electronic communication, where practical.
○ Delegate time for administrative duties, such as making and responding to telephone calls, writing reports and letters, analysing data, maintaining an overview of policy and practice.
○ Obtain clerical support wherever possible for minuting meetings, collating information for annual reviews and statutory assessment referrals, word-processing reports, updating records, organizing materials, filing, etc.
○ Organize files so that they are easily accessible to relevant staff.
○ Maintain individual pupil files with appropriate current information.
○ Make available an SEN handbook with relevant proformas and easy-to-follow instructions.

LIST 12
Good communication

Good communication is the key to gaining cooperation from all parties involved in meeting the needs of pupils with SEN.

Coordination in school

○ Hold regular meetings as appropriate.
○ Use existing school meetings, such as staff meetings, briefings and departmental meetings, to collect and disseminate information.
○ Use the intranet, staffroom noticeboards, pigeonholes or trays and staff circulars.
○ Use communication routes, such as curriculum 'link' teachers, teaching assistants and learning mentors, to collect and disseminate information.
○ Establish a regular cycle of meetings to liaise with the designated governor for SEN, or the governing body, with regard to aspects of SEN.
○ Make parent- and pupil-friendly information available.

Coordination with external agencies

○ Use the common assessment framework and other communication systems set up by children's services.
○ Have a good knowledge of the personnel and their role in the organization.
○ Make sure you have a clear understanding of the services offered by individual agencies.
○ Identify points for planning and targets from the external agency at the time of their visit, pending the receipt of a report.
○ Forward plan for meetings, and contact relevant personnel in good time.
○ Try to work cooperatively with feeder and receiving schools, local authority support services and the local special schools.

Coordination with parents

○ Seek parents' views regularly and remember to share and celebrate pupils' successes.

○ Utilize both formal and informal opportunities for liaison, for example:
  - contact through the keyworker
  - meetings by appointment as appropriate
  - the use of home–school link books
  - written and telephone communications.
○ Hold a regular or occasional SEN 'surgery'.
○ Hold workshops.
○ Encourage parents to help in school.
○ Use parents' evenings as part of the review process.

Forging home–school links

Working with SEN pupils, it is essential to have the understanding and support of the parents and carers. There is a lot you can do to make them feel involved.

❍ Make sure parents have a copy of all relevant policies and documents.

❍ Ensure parents are informed about provision made for their child and changes in provision. Take time to explain exactly what support a child is receiving, when this takes place and how progress will be monitored.

❍ Check that parents have copies of individual education plans and details regarding any help and support.

❍ Make sure that parents and carers have given permission and know times and dates of visits by other agencies.

❍ Make sure parents and carers know the names of staff who work with their child individually.

❍ Invite parents into school to meet the people who are involved with their child.

❍ Have available contact numbers for support groups and agencies that offer advice.

❍ Ask parents what strategies they use at home to help their child.

❍ Ask parents and carers if they would like some suggestions for what they can do at home.

❍ At meetings, make sure parents and carers have chance to give their views – even if they do not always correspond with the school's points of view.

❍ Encourage parents into school to discuss their concerns and, as schools can be busy environments, provide parents with a list of days and times when staff can be contacted.

Effective provision for pupils

To ensure that there is effective SEN provision for all pupils who need it, the following procedures should be in place in schools:

- Provision maps (see List 66).
- Quality teaching in all classrooms ensures an inclusive environment and meets the needs of all pupils.
- Pupils' needs are accurately identified by school staff and appropriate provision is made.
- Teachers have high expectations of pupils' progress and set realistic but challenging targets.
- Relevant assessments are carried out.
- Pupil progress is monitored and reviewed.
- Identified pupils have an individual pupil plan.
- All who have knowledge of the pupil contribute to the individual pupil plans as appropriate.
- The SENCO maintains an overview of the process, ensures consistency and provides advice, but all teachers should be teachers of special needs.
- The SENCO oversees the implementation of individual pupil plans.
- Appropriate records and documentation of provision are maintained, with reference to local authority guidance.
- Pupils are included in the decision-making process and their views are given status.

LIST 15 Continuing professional development

The SEN scene is constantly changing, with new initiatives coming on stream. It is essential for staff to keep up to date with these changes. Here are some ideas for how you can do this and support the continuing professional development (CPD) of all staff.

For the SENCO

- ○ Maintain and update your knowledge and skills.
- ○ Liaise with other SENCOs through cluster or pyramid groups and SENCO support groups to establish effective networks.
- ○ Join a relevant professional organization.
- ○ Take regular opportunities to share information.

For the staff

- ○ Identify the training needs of all staff.
- ○ Organize and coordinate INSET on SEN issues to be delivered by other professionals.
- ○ Lead INSET where appropriate – this may include working parties.
- ○ Disseminate information, such as the recommendations of the Code of Practice, local authority guidance or the school's own SEN policy and practice.
- ○ Ensure that all teaching assistants are aware of the training and qualifications structure.
- ○ Collaborate and problem-solve with colleagues on issues relating to SEN.
- ○ Use resources for the support of SEN to best effect.
- ○ Display and circulate leaflets, articles, journals, etc.
- ○ Provide opportunities for staff to observe colleagues and visit other schools in order to share good practice.

Diary for the start of the school year

- Consult educational psychologists, pupil services, support services and Connexions (if relevant) on annual and transitional review dates.
- Enter annual review dates on the calendar and in the diary.
- Enter examination dates on the calendar and dates for submission of access arrangements.
- Update provision maps.
- Set individual education plan review dates with relevant members of staff and parents.
- Plan the in-service training schedule (this may include formal or informal training opportunities).
- Set dates for teaching assistant performance management meetings.
- Plan a meeting schedule (internal, school liaison, between colleagues).
- Contact outside agencies.
- Inform parents of changes to the nature of their child's SEN provision.

LIST 17 Diary for the end of the school year

○ Request end-of-year test scores (literacy and numeracy) for all pupils (primary) or targeted groups (secondary) and any other data to indicate progress.

○ Analyse test results to inform planning for SEN.

○ Allocate support for the next academic year.

○ Write support timetables.

○ Support teachers in writing individual pupil support programmes.

○ In secondary schools, write and distribute pupil information on SEN to support staff and receiving teachers, subject team leaders and/or heads of year, attaching highlighted provision maps.

○ In primary schools, ensure that information is passed on to the relevant teachers and inform staff of the needs of new entrants.

○ Liaise with the SENCOs of partner schools and early years settings. Transfer relevant information to Connexions and FE sector (Year 11 pupils and above).

○ Organize pupil records for transfer.

○ Review the SEN handbook in preparation for the next academic year.

Other tasks for the diary

- Plan new or adjust existing pupil support programmes.
- Adjust SEN records and organization of pupil files.
- Update SEN timetables for teachers and teaching assistants.
- Plan observations of teaching assistants.
- Update or adjust essential proformas (administrative framework) and the SEN handbook.
- Undertake informal monitoring of pupil support.
- Liaise with colleagues, external agencies and parents.
- Undertake individual pupil assessments – if necessary class and subject teachers should be able to provide you with detailed information on needs and progress.
- Undertake individual pupil reviews with the keyworker (including an annual review of statemented pupils).
- Consider internal and external examination requirements, including SATs and GCSE.

Twice a year

- Review SEN records.
- Work with relevant members of staff to update pupil progress.
- Support teachers in undertaking the IEP review process.
- Liaise with the SEN governor.
- Undertake tasks identified on the SEN development plan.

Annually or periodically

- Review and revise the SEN development plan.
- Review the SEN policy.
- Undertake a self-review and an evaluation of SEN provision.
- Undertake a department review, including data analysis.
- Prepare the report to governors and to parents.
- Discuss the accessibility plan with the senior management team and governors.

L I S T 19 Ten commandments for stress reduction

- Thou shalt not be perfect, or even try to be.
- Thou shalt not try to be all things to all people.
- Thou shalt sometimes leave things undone.
- Thou shalt not spread thyself too thin.
- Thou shalt learn to say 'no'.
- Thou shalt schedule time for thyself and for thy support network.
- Thou shalt switch thyself off, and do nothing – regularly.
- Thou shalt not even feel guilty for doing nothing, or saying 'no'.
- Thou shalt be boring, untidy, inelegant, and unattractive at times.
- Especially, thou shalt not be thine own worst enemy. But, be thine own best friend.

Classroom Management

LIST 20 Organizing the environment

It is often the SENCO's role to advise others on classroom management as it is especially important that the basic essentials are in place for pupils with SEN. These pupils often find less structured environments very difficult, so it's worth planning ahead to organize the learning environment.

○ Ensure that the classroom is ordered and tidy, with equipment clearly labelled.
○ Develop a system for keeping track of work, such as an individual folder or file.
○ Ensure that work is appropriate for a pupil's attention span.
○ Provide clear, specific instructions about task requirements, supported by pictures or diagrams.
○ Be clear about expectations for movement around the room.
○ Establish routines for the start and end of lessons.
○ Prepare pupils in advance for changes in activity or the end of lessons, and use visual props if necessary.
○ Use agreed signals to maintain attention, for example, whole-class signals for everyone and signals for individual children that might be agreed in advance.
○ Seat the pupil away from busy areas or windows in order to avoid distractions.
○ Seat the pupil in close proximity to the teacher, if appropriate.
○ Seat pupils near good role models.
○ Try a range of seating arrangements, for example, provide small group tables and more formal rows for independent work. A horse-shoe arrangement can promote discussion and also independent work.
○ Consider paired work and learning partners, with children working together on particular tasks.
○ Have a quiet area or independent study area set aside.

Lessons

Your role will be a lot easier if all teachers manage their classrooms effectively. Here are a few tips for making lessons more accessible for pupils with SEN.

○ Provide a summary of the lesson.
○ Actively involve pupils in lessons. Encourage them to help in the lesson presentation, supporting the teacher in using the smart board or demonstrating practical tasks.
○ Provide a range of activities during lessons in order to maintain attention and interest.
○ Ensure that the pupil is managing to keep up with the pace of lessons and that they have managed to complete one task before you move on to the next.
○ Be aware that pupils might have difficulty with multi-tasking, e.g. trying to listen to a lesson presentation and writing down information at the same time.
○ Avoid overlong verbal presentations and (at least) ensure they are supported with practical demonstrations and visual cues.
○ Check with pupils that they have understood task requirements – ask them to repeat instructions to check for understanding.
○ Support written instructions by highlighting key sections and key words.
○ Provide the pupil with their own list of written instructions, as opposed to asking them to copy from a board or smart board.
○ Make regular eye contact with the pupil.
○ Avoid the use of over fussy and detailed worksheets. Keep them simple – only use pictures and visual cues that are needed and use a clear font.
○ Keep written and verbal instructions short.
○ Highlight key sections on worksheets with a border, bold text or colour.
○ Ensure that staff have frequent contact with the pupil during the lesson.
○ Encourage pupils to ask for help when needed rather than imposing staff upon them.
○ Encourage pupils to use a variety of recording techniques, such as tape recorders, computers and diagrams.

- Ensure that pupils are rewarded and praised for task completion and effort.
- Encourage pupils to make frequent responses throughout lessons, e.g. encouraging individual or group responses and the use of all non-verbal responses such as hands up, head nods.
- Vary the type of activity within lessons, e.g. role-playing cooperative learning activities, game-type activities.

Behaviour management

Pupils with SEN can be very challenging, but poor behaviour in the classroom can usually be avoided by following these general rules.

○ Be consistent.

○ Stick to routines.

○ Communicate clearly with pupils.

○ Try to avoid confrontations.

○ Reward and pay attention to good behaviour.

○ Ignore some behaviours – don't pick up on the small things.

○ Develop individual plans and contracts with pupils, if needed. Encourage pupils to set targets and monitor their own behaviour. Focus on targets that can be achieved and limit them to one or two behaviours at a time. Provide frequent, positive feedback on progress.

○ Identify one or two specific behaviours to focus on, e.g. staying in the seat, putting hands up, walking, not running, down the corridors.

○ Plan for times that are difficult for pupils, e.g. breaktimes, movement between rooms, lining up.

○ Provide frequent reminders of expected behaviour.

○ Be aware of the onset of possible problems and divert pupils to an alternative task.

○ Provide a range of strategies that the pupil could follow if he/she needs to wait for the attention of an adult.

○ Use visual cues to remind pupils to focus on the task – a traffic light system with cards showing the colours green, amber, red can be used. When the class or child is on task, a green card can be shown and appropriate praise given. Showing the orange card provides a reminder to focus on task, and when the pupil is back on task, praise can be given. A red card can be used where the pupil has not resumed work and a sanction is then applied.

○ Focus on improving behaviour around the school environment as well as in the classroom by using a reward system across the school and encouraging other staff to take part in the reward-giving process.

Rewards and sanctions

Rewards can be a very powerful tool for managing behaviour. Children tend to respond positively to praise and rewards, whereas sanctions are less effective, so try and use them sparingly.

- Have classroom rules that are clear, specific and simple, but don't have too many!
- Encourage pupils to agree what the rules should be. Discuss and review the rules frequently, adapting them if necessary. Make sure they understand what happens if they break the rules.
- Remember to change the rewards frequently. Strategies used to motivate a child can lose their effectiveness quickly, so a range of rewards will need to be available.
- Reward and praise specific behaviours immediately, e.g. try 'well done for putting your hand up to ask a question', rather than simply saying 'good, well done'.
- Make sure you give rewards commonly used throughout the school.
- Use smiles, eye contact, stickers and stars – these usually go down well as rewards.
- Ensure that sanctions are consistently applied to all pupils.
- Avoid using sanctions for the whole class based on the behaviour of an individual pupil.
- Try using reprimands and the loss of small privileges as effective sanctions.
- Use 'time out' (removing the pupil from the room) but have a graduated response with a warning system and be consistent when using it. Also remember that pupils need to be supervised.
- Remember, rewards are more powerful than sanctions in changing behaviour.

Managing individuals

○ Give the pupil the opportunity to apologize or take back what they have said – this can stop a situation escalating.

○ Control your own anger – if you don't you will lose authority.

○ Be polite at all times.

○ Avoid being drawn into arguments as it takes away from what is being said and is undignified.

○ Find out facts instead of jumping to conclusions.

○ Don't threaten at the first sign of a problem – a graduated response is needed.

○ Treat each pupil fairly, otherwise they will lose respect for you.

○ Stick to the point you want to make and don't get sidetracked. Repeat your point firmly, several times if necessary.

○ Avoid negative body language – folding arms, finger-wagging, towering over pupils.

○ Avoid making sarcastic or patronising remarks – it is rude and sets a negative example.

○ Don't shout – it just adds to the general commotion and can indicate a lack of control.

○ Speak to students away from friends and classmates – this avoids making them feel silly and also stops friends joining in.

Individual Special Needs

LIST 25

Attention deficit hyperactivity disorder: general indicators

Attention deficit hyperactivity disorder (ADHD) can co-exist with other conditions, such as dyslexia, speech and language difficulties, coordination difficulties, conduct disorder and Tourettes syndrome. Some children are not hyperactive but are often referred to as having attention deficit disorder (ADD).

It is important to remember that many of the behaviours associated with ADHD can be found in most children at one time or other and when diagnosing ADHD it is the frequency, intensity and developmental characteristics that need to be considered.

Impulsivity

- Has difficulty waiting in turn in groups.
- Leaves activities incomplete.
- Interrupts and shouts out.
- Gets into dangerous situations or activities without considering the consequences.

Over-activity

- Fidgets or always appears to be 'on the go'.
- Has difficulty remaining in a seat.
- Is easily distracted and has difficulty settling to task or completing task.

Inattention

- Makes careless mistakes in work.
- Has problems organizing him/herself to do tasks.
- Forgets instructions and daily routines, loses equipment.

Parents and carers might tell you that their child:

○ has a tendency to be a restless sleeper
○ exhibits a pattern of fussy feeding from nursing through to solid
  foods
○ never stops and is 'like a whirlwind'
○ is easily frustrated
○ butts into conversations
○ always needs instant gratification.

See Chapter 7 for strategies that are useful for supporting pupils
with ADHD.

LIST 26 ADHD: stimulant medication

The most frequently used drugs to treat children with ADHD are Ritalin (Methylphenidate) and Dexamphetamine, but the use of medication alone is not recommended and is not the cure. It can, however, help the child to be less impulsive and inattentive.

The drugs are:

○ stimulants not sedatives
○ short acting – usually lasting between three and five hours
○ usually given in either two or three doses during the day
○ used from around the age of five and upwards
○ not addictive.

Side effects can include:

○ loss of appetite
○ difficulty sleeping
○ slight slowing of growth
○ feeling sad.

Medication often needs administering in school around lunchtime, and it is important to follow the appropriate procedures. All drugs should be stored safely and securely – your school should have a policy relating to medication.

LIST 27 Autistic spectrum disorders

Autism and Asperger's syndrome are both autistic spectrum disorders (ASDs). They share three common diagnostic features:

○ Difficulties in communication
○ Difficulties with social relationships
○ Lack of imagination and creative play.

Autism

Characteristics are usually noticeable by the age of three or younger. Communication can be very restricted; sometimes speech does not develop or is much delayed and characterized by echolalia (repeated phrases), repetitive questioning and peculiarities of tone and grammar. The child can have difficulty communicating his/her needs. Augmentative communication systems, such as signs and visual symbols, are needed in order to communicate, e.g. the Picture Exchange Communication System (PECS).

The child:

○ can often appear indifferent and aloof to others
○ often has significant learning difficulties
○ often needs highly structured intensive programmes with high levels of adult support.

Asperger's syndrome

Although more common than autism, this is often diagnosed later and needs are not always as easily identified, sometimes only becoming apparent when higher level social skills and communication skills are needed.

The child:

○ is often delayed in developing speech. Grammar usually develops along normal developmental lines but there are difficulties with pragmatics (the use of language in a social context), semantics (meanings) and prosody (stress, rhythm and pitch)
○ often has poor non-verbal communication
○ often wants to communicate but has difficulty with social rules

32

o does not have the severe learning difficulties associated with autism and often has average and above abilities.

Remember, children with autism and Asperger's syndrome are children first and they will all have individual and unique characteristics.

LIST 28 ASD: general characteristics

Most children with ASD are diagnosed before starting school or very early in their school life, but if not there are some general characteristics you might observe in children whose difficulties are at the milder end of the continuum, or those with Asperger's syndrome.

Communication

○ Difficulty repairing a conversation.
○ Confused by over literal phrases, such as 'pull your socks up', 'looks can kill', 'change your mind', 'it's raining cats and dogs'.
○ Limited variation in tone and expression.
○ Difficulty understanding metaphors.
○ Overly formal speech.
○ Often talks at length on a topic.

Social relationships

○ Often likes contact with others but has problems with non-verbal signs and facial expressions.
○ Often indifferent to the interests and activities of his/her peer group.
○ Difficulty making and maintaining appropriate eye contact.
○ Shows a lack of empathy.

Imagination

○ Often engages in solitary play.
○ Play is often a replay or copied, e.g. from a film or real-life event.
○ Takes on the role of an object rather than a person, sometimes related to the child's special interest, e.g. trains.
○ Thinking can be rigid.
○ Difficulty generalizing learning to other situations.

Interests and routines

○ Likes to make collections of objects.
○ Has favourite topics of special interest, such as transport or science.

- Can develop routines, such as lining things up or carrying out tasks in a particular way.

Problems with motor coordination

- Not unique to people with ASD and many children experience difficulties in this area.

Sensory sensitivity

- Sensitivity to touching, unexpected noises, textures, tastes, smells.

ASD: including and supporting pupils

○ Ensure all staff in school receive appropriate training.
○ Get to know each pupil's likes and dislikes, strengths and weaknesses. Ask the parent or carer, as they will have an in-depth knowledge of their child.
○ Recognize that changes in behaviour might reflect anxiety.
○ Try to keep routines the same.
○ Prepare pupils for change.
○ Plan transitions to the next school and next class carefully and don't forget to involve the pupil and parent or carer.
○ Use a visual timetable or daily plan so that the pupil knows what to do next.
○ Break down instructions for tasks and support them with visual cues or clear written instructions.
○ Remember that specific times of the school day might be trigger points and will need planning for carefully – PE, particular curriculum areas, lunchtime, wet breaktimes, assembly, visitors, such as a music or theatre company.
○ Use visual props, pictures and objects.
○ Be aware of the environment and how this might cause anxiety for the child. For example, changes in the organization of furniture, noises such as the grass being cut outside or building work in school.
○ Reduce distractions and provide a quiet area for working.
○ Help the child to practise new skills in different environments.

ASD: special interests, communication and social skills

Dealing with a pupil's special interest

o Ensure there is controlled access, and be careful if the interest is dangerous.

o Use it for a constructive purpose, e.g. in the curriculum – counting dinosaurs, sorting into large and small, researching and writing a project using ICT.

o Be positive – some special interests can form future careers and occupations.

Communicating with pupils

o Keep instructions clear and specific.

o Say the pupil's name so that they know an instruction applies to them – the child may not be aware that the term 'everybody' includes them.

o Give one instruction at a time, or break lengthy instructions down into smaller parts.

o Avoid instructions that contain the word 'don't'. Instead of 'don't run' use 'John, walk'.

o Praise good behaviour.

o Avoid 'would you like' and provide clear choices, e.g. painting or Lego.

o Give the pupil time to respond to requests and instructions.

o Avoid sarcasm – this is not good with any child.

o Avoid idioms.

o Keep facial expressions and non-verbal signals clear and simple.

o Use positive, not negative, statements.

o Support instructions with visual cues if necessary.

o If the child is upset or there is a problem, keep language to a minimum as they might calm more quickly.

Social interaction and play skills

o Teach the skills of social interaction.

o Model appropriate behaviour.

o Use social skills programmes.

o Use social stories such as *My Social Stories Book* by Carol Gray, Abbie Leigh White, Sean McAndrew (Jessica Kingsley, 2002)

o Use drama and role-play.

o Use video and audio methods.

ASD: breaktimes and lunchtimes

Pupils with ASD might be easily influenced by others and behave inappropriately, so you will need to teach and model acceptable behaviour and language for this time.

○ If the pupil is isolated, particularly from sporting activities and imaginative play games, use a 'circle of friends' approach, and pair the pupil with a child with whom they get along well.

○ Have opportunities for independent activities. Respect that the pupil does not always want to be forced into being part of the crowd. Activities such as computer time or time engaged in their particular interest are appropriate as long as there are time limits imposed and they are combined with opportunities to develop social activities and interact with others.

○ Provide a safe haven for wet breaktimes – this might be an area of the classroom or another room with fewer pupils around.

○ Provide opportunities for structured indoor and outdoor activities, ball games, board games, ICT, construction toys. This will help reduce repetitive and restricted self-stimulatory behaviours.

○ Make clear rules for breaktimes, supported by visual reminders.

○ Let the pupil know which staff member is on duty at breaktimes, lunchtime and after school.

○ At lunchtime, consider the best place to sit the pupil – if it's very noisy, find a quieter area.

○ Inform lunchtime staff of any particular dietary requirements, taste or texture sensitivities relating to food and drink. Involve staff if a particular programme is being followed regarding diet or trying out new food.

L I S T 32 Developmental dyspraxia: general indicators

Developmental dyspraxia, sometimes called developmental coordination disorder (DCD), is generally recognized as an impairment or immaturity of the organization of movement. There can also be associated problems of language perception and thought. There are some general indicators which show up at different ages.

Ages 3–5

○ Difficulty with activities such as peddling a tricycle.
○ High levels of motor activity, never seeming to stay in one place, with constant movement of hands and feet.
○ Awkward gait when running and walking.
○ Avoids physical activities at playtime.
○ Avoids Lego and other construction toys.
○ Poor pencil grip, problems using scissors and threading beads.
○ Limited play skills – does not join in, preferring adult company.
○ Limited concentration on tasks, visiting activities for a short time and leaving activities unfinished.
○ Problems copying from a board.

Older children – Key Stages 1 and 2

○ Difficulties with motor activities persist and become more noticeable.
○ Difficulty in dressing and undressing and learning to tie shoelaces.
○ Slow, immature, uneven written work.
○ Difficulty developing reading and spelling.
○ Difficulty with concentrating and listening, often appearing off task.
○ Immature drawing and avoidance of art activities.
○ Often slow to respond to verbal instructions and give a verbal response.
○ Continued difficulties developing social skills and often appears isolated.
○ Some children report physical difficulties, such as migraines, headaches and feeling sick.

Teenagers

o Many earlier difficulties persist.
o Difficulty with physical activities and often avoids them.
o Getting organized in lessons can be challenging.
o Work is often incomplete.
o Often thought of as not attending or listening in lessons.
o Can become more isolated from his/her peer group.

LIST 33 — Developmental dyspraxia: including and supporting pupils

Where appropriate, pupils should have activities differentiated and access to the programmes and additional support of the National Numeracy and Literacy Strategies. Some pupils will require IEPs at either School Action or, with advice from outside agencies, School Action Plus of the Code of Practice. A small number of pupils will have a statement of SEN.

Some pupils will also benefit from access to structured fine and gross motor programmes that should ideally be carried out on a daily basis for between 15 and 30 minutes. Children do not necessarily need the programmes to be ongoing.

Helping with writing

- Provide access to handwriting programmes.
- Use alternative methods of recording.
- Do not ask the pupil to copy from the board.
- Ask the pupil to choose pens and pencils with which they are comfortable.
- Use guidelines for writing.
- Trial a range of paper for recording on, use larger scale paper and encourage larger scale writing until writing patterns are established.
- Begin by writing on a vertical surface and use large-scale lined paper in order to develop up-and-down and left-and-right progression skills.
- Ensure that the pupil is in the best writing position, with appropriate positioning, such as a sloping surface on which to write.
- Make sure pupils sit with their bottoms at the back of the chair and with their feet on the ground, body and head upright, forearms supported.
- Differentiate homework tasks accordingly.

Developmental dyspraxia: other ways to help

○ Encourage oral contributions and presentations as an alternative to some written work.

○ Support the pupil in being organized for tasks. Perhaps produce a visual prompt card or a short written list of the essential requirements for particular tasks.

○ Provide the pupil with additional time for getting dressed and undressed during PE.

○ Use writing and speaking frames for organizing and structuring work.

○ Help the pupil to sequence pictures and write a few short sentences about the story created.

○ Set targets with the pupil about what they might achieve in a lesson. Pupils will quickly become demotivated if they are never able to complete tasks.

○ Use computer software programs to improve planning and organizational skills.

○ Consider using visual timetables for pupils with organizational difficulties.

○ Provide pupils with opportunities to revisit and reinforce basic concepts.

○ Plan transitions carefully.

Dyslexia: general indicators

Many children will experience difficulties developing literacy skills, but for the dyslexic pupil many of their difficulties persist, often when additional support has been provided. Difficulties in the following areas are often observed.

Reading

○ Slow to develop reading.
○ Often has a weak knowledge of alphabetical order.
○ Rereads text to comprehend.
○ Confuses similar looking letters, such as b/d, and groups of letters, ch/sh.
○ Relies on context or picture clues.

Spelling

○ Difficulty writing individual letters, which are often poorly formed.
○ Continues to reverse letters above the age of eight.
○ Confuses the order of letters in words – said as siad
○ Spells the same words differently in one sample of writing.
○ Adds letters to words and over applies spelling rules – whas instead of was.

Written work

○ Misses out words in a sentence or adds words.
○ Limited punctuation and grammar skills.
○ Writing is slow and laboured, often with many crossings out.
○ Work contains letter reversals with b, d and u (many young children do this but with pupils with dyslexia this persists into Key Stage 2 and beyond).

Maths

Problems with:

○ number bonds and tables
○ time
○ mental arithmetic sums
○ remembering symbols
○ remembering direction of working.

Social, emotional and behaviour

○ Can have low self-esteem, particularly as they progress through school and their difficulties become more apparent to themselves and their peers.
○ Avoids literacy activities.

Strengths

○ Often has good visual spatial skills. Younger children might be good with construction and drawing; older children with drawing, model-making and ICT.
○ Can be a creative thinker and able to see solutions to problems.
○ Good long-term memory.

LIST 36   Dyslexia: identification and provision

Dyslexia is common within primary and secondary school, therefore identifying children should be part of general good teaching practice rather than reliant on specialist assessment and diagnosis, although this should be called on when children do not make progress despite appropriate programmes and strategies.

As part of an inclusion agenda within school, it is useful if all staff have an awareness of dyslexia so that pupils' needs can be identified and appropriate programmes put in place. In making an assessment within school, the following information/assessment could be considered as a starting point:

- Use of National Curriculum assessments.
- Use of standardized or non-standardized literacy assessments.
- Interviews and discussions with pupils to determine their views, learning style and social and emotional functioning. (Many pupils with dyslexia develop low self-esteem and some develop behaviour difficulties. Determining learning style is also important in order that appropriate programmes are put in place.)
- Discussion with parents.
- Analysis and observation of the environment.

What is assessed?

- Phonological awareness
- Reading accuracy and fluency
- Spelling
- Writing
- Comprehension
- Attitudes and feelings about literacy
- Whether the school is inclusive of dyslexic pupils.

Suitable provision

- Programmes, such as those recommended at Wave 2 and 3 of the National Literacy Strategy (see List 78 Literacy intervention).
- An IEP with SMART (Specific, Measurable, Achievable,

Relevant and Time-related) targets in order that progress and intervention can be monitored.

○ A dyslexia-friendly school approach.

Checklist for a dyslexia-friendly school

- School has a dyslexia policy.
- Parents and carers are informed of the policy.
- Parents and carers are involved in helping pupils develop literacy.
- Parents and carers are informed of progress.
- An information booklet for parents is available.
- All staff have awareness training in dyslexia.
- Teaching staff have received training in teaching dyslexic pupils.
- At least one person has an additional qualification in specific learning difficulties.
- An information booklet for pupils is available.
- Resources for supporting and helping dyslexic pupils are available throughout the school.
- A range of alternative recording strategies is used, such as mind-maps and writing frames.
- A range of reading material is available, suitable for age and reading level.
- Spelling is supported through ACE spelling dictionaries and handheld spellcheckers.
- ICT is used for recording and planning work.
- Pupils with dyslexia are identified in a systematic way.
- Provision for dyslexic pupils, such as programmes suggested at Wave 2 and 3, is clearly identified.
- There are clear entry and exit criteria for additional individual and/or small-group support.
- Programmes provided reflect a comprehensive approach to literacy development, and:
  - are based on multi-sensory approaches
  - take into account learning styles of individuals
  - are based on mastery learning
  - use a range of groupings.
- Pupils are involved in target setting and monitoring progress.
- There is a marking policy, such as correcting those words which are nearly right, but not correcting more than five errors.

LIST 38   Dyslexia: including and supporting pupils

Dyslexic pupils should be supported through differentiation of the curriculum and through the Wave 1, 2 and 3 provision available as part of the National Numeracy and National Literacy Strategies. Additional small-group and individual support might also be needed for some pupils, in which case they should have an IEP at School Action or School Action Plus if other agencies have been involved. Some, but very few, pupils will need a statement of SEN.

Dyslexia-friendly school approaches should be part of whole-school planning. In addition to individual programmes, you can also help generally with reading.

Reading

○ Consider the readability of the text – too many errors and the pupil will soon switch off and will not fully comprehend. Consider abridged texts and those with age-appropriate material but with text at an earlier level.
○ Avoid asking pupils to read aloud without adequate time to prepare.
○ Put pupils in pairs for working.
○ Use taped or computer-based texts for some subjects.
○ Ensure worksheets are differentiated for pupils.
○ Highlight key words and instructions on worksheets to help with comprehension.
○ Provide regular opportunities for paired and shared reading.
○ Consider arrangements in examinations – some pupils might need a reader.

Dyslexia: presenting written work

- ○ Allow the pupil to present work on tape or verbally.
- ○ Provide help sheets for written work containing key vocabulary or phrases.
- ○ Use computer programs.
- ○ Use writing frames to help the pupil plan their ideas and structure their work.
- ○ Consider the use of a scribe for some assessment purposes, although pupils need to work as independently as possible. Paired and group work can be used, with pupils with good literacy skills doing the recording of work.
- ○ Where possible, photocopy notes rather than have the pupil copying.
- ○ Give the pupil the opportunity to use labelled drawings, diagrams and pictures to record information.
- ○ Evaluate written work on content rather than presentation. Identify targets for improvement but make sure these are kept to a realistic number to prevent the pupil becoming demotivated.
- ○ Give homework out on written sheets so that the pupil is not having to copy down information.
- ○ Differentiate homework so that the pupil is able to have some free time and is not spending more time than their peers completing homework.
- ○ Value verbal contributions to lessons.

Planning and organisation

- ○ Provide the pupil with a weekly timetable, supported by visual cues if needed.
- ○ Provide support for developing study skills.
- ○ Create opportunities for regular home–school liaison to ensure messages reach home.

LIST 40 Dyslexia: spelling

In addition to a structured spelling programme, the following should be considered:

○ Provide students with a personal spelling dictionary which contains key words from a range of subjects and topics.
○ Provide pupils with a list of words which they have particular difficulty spelling.
○ Make computer spellcheck facilities available and consider using portable spellcheckers, such as the Franklin spellchecker, if the pupil is not able to identify their own spelling errors.
○ Teach the pupil to use an ACE Spelling Dictionary if appropriate but don't forget this requires the pupil to analyse sounds in words.
○ Display frequently used words in the classroom.

LIST 41 Dyslexia: building self-esteem

Low self-esteem is demotivating, especially for those with a specific learning difficulty, as they face obstacles in numerous areas. There are some simple strategies which will help to enhance a pupil's self-esteem and increase their confidence.

○ Acknowledge the pupil's difficulties and include them in target setting and monitoring progress.
○ Use strategies such as dyslexia-friendly school approaches to help a pupil feel part of the classroom and school environment.
○ Focus on the pupil's verbal contributions and strengths.
○ Ensure targets set are SMART (Specific, Measurable, Achievable, Relevant and Time-related) so that the pupil is able to achieve.
○ Use reward systems recognizing a variety of achievements.
○ Praise success.

LIST 42 Hearing impairment: general indicators

Deaf is the term that is generally used among the deaf community and includes all types of hearing loss. For many children their hearing loss has been identified before they begin school and a range of support has already been implemented through education and health services. Often children will have a statement of SEN. There are several children, however, who have not been identified prior to school or develop a condition after starting school. The following checklist might be useful to identify common indicators:

○ Does not appear to hear or respond when his/her name is called.
○ Asks regularly for instructions to be repeated.
○ Appears to misunderstand or ignore instructions or questions.
○ Appears to daydream.
○ Watches faces closely.
○ Rarely participates or volunteers information at class discussion times.
○ Often nods or shakes the head rather than saying yes or no (often inappropriately).
○ Might speak quietly or appear to talk loudly and shout.
○ Has noticeable difficulties with speech production.
○ Displays an immature vocabulary.
○ Is often withdrawn and quiet.
○ Can have difficulty developing social skills and friendships.
○ Displays behaviour difficulties.
○ Is slow to develop reading skills, and has problems developing phonic skills and sound discrimination.
○ Suffers from frequent colds and ear infections with discharges.
○ Has parents or siblings with hearing impairments.

What to do next

○ Ask the parents whether they have similar concerns and discuss how the pupil is at home.
○ With the parents' permission, refer the pupil for a hearing test. The parents might do this through the health service or often the appropriate service for children with a hearing impairment can offer advice or make arrangements for assessment.

L I S T 43   Hearing impairment: including and supporting pupils

○ If the pupil wears hearing aids, ensure that he/she is wearing them and that they are switched on.

○ With radio aids, only use them when talking to a pupil either individually or within a small group.

○ Make sure that you have gained the pupil's attention – visually or physically.

○ Make sure that the pupil has a good seating position, where they are able to see you when you are talking or other pupils when they are talking. The front is not always best – to the side and towards the middle can be better.

○ Ensure the pupil is not sitting next to doors or windows where there can be distractions.

○ Introduce subjects at the start of a session and clearly identify changes in subjects.

○ Use visual cues and present information in a wide variety of ways, through pictures, diagrams, notes and videos.

○ Write new and key words on the board.

○ Remember that some pupils will require additional explanation prior to the start of lessons and additional follow up at the end of sessions.

○ Don't speak with your back to the pupil – they won't be able to lip-read.

○ Make sure your lip patterns are clear but don't exaggerate them. Try to keep a normal rhythm to your speech.

○ Don't shout.

○ Speak at the level of the pupil so they can see you clearly – bend down if necessary.

○ Try to keep background noise to a minimum when speaking to a pupil.

○ Try to keep in one place when talking to the pupil.

○ Check that instructions have been understood.

○ Don't stand with your back to the light.

○ Consider using gestures to support or back up communication.

○ Make sure that all staff who teach the pupil have information regarding the nature of their hearing impairment and appropriate strategies and teaching methods.

○ Enable staff to receive deaf-awareness training.

○ Ensure that role models include deaf or hearing-impaired people.

LIST 44 Visual impairment: general indicators

Visual impairment is a term applied to a range of conditions. It can be hereditary or acquired through an illness or accident or the ageing process. Many children with a visual impairment are identified at a preschool age, often soon after birth or within the first few weeks. By the time they get to school a range of support has often been implemented through education and health services, working with parents and carers. However, some children might experience difficulties later on in life. If you are concerned about a child's vision speak to parents/carers:

○ discuss having an assessment of vision – an eye test
○ contact the service for pupils with visual impairment who will advise as to what steps you might take.

Use this list of common indicators to help identify pupils with visual problems.

○ Clumsy and reluctant to engage in PE lessons and physical activities.
○ Excessive head movements.
○ Lack of concentration on tasks.
○ Weeping or runny eyes.
○ Headaches.
○ Discomfort with glare and brightness.
○ Startled responses to movement.
○ Misses things when picking up objects or putting them down.
○ Seems isolated and withdrawn.
○ Holds books or written material too close or too far away.
○ Peers towards the board, whiteboard or computer screen.

Visual impairment: including and supporting pupils

Many pupils will have programmes in place detailing individual arrangements and these should be followed and reviewed along with staff involved, parents and carers.

○ Ensure close liaison with parents and carers.
○ Know a pupil's strengths and weaknesses and focus on the strengths.
○ Know who is working with the pupil and when, including teaching assistants, advisory staff and mobility staff.
○ Become familiar with what equipment and adaptations the pupil needs and ensure that all staff who work with the pupil have a list of requirements.
○ Check that any equipment is working.
○ Remember that pupils with a visual impairment might need more direct teaching of concepts that other children pick up on easily.
○ Engage in practical demonstrations and activities where possible.
○ Don't ask the pupil to copy from blackboards, and be aware that whiteboards and interactive screens might be problematic.
○ If possible, give the pupil their own copy of written material.

Seating/writing position

○ Be aware of the pupil's seating position in the class and ask them what is best for them – it may be at the front, to the side or away from the window. Curtains or blinds for windows are often necessary.
○ Stand away from the window as glare might affect pupil's ability to see.
○ Provide individual lighting if necessary.
○ Make sure the seat and desk are at the correct height.
○ If the pupil needs to adopt an unusual working position due to the nature of their visual impairment, don't discourage them but be mindful that they might become tired and need a rest.

Storage

○ Equipment should be stored in a place accessible for the pupil wherever possible, so that they retain their independence.

○ Pupils should be told and shown where key equipment is stored in classroom.

○ Labels on equipment should also be appropriate for a pupil with visual impairment.

LIST 46
Visual impairment: in the classroom

○ Address the pupil directly – say his or her name to gain attention.

○ Be specific with instructions, especially directions.

○ Provide additional time for the completion of written work.

○ Make sure the pupil has the correct writing equipment – pens and pencils of various widths and high contrasting colours.

○ Check worksheets for suitable font type and size, ink colour, uncluttered layout and spacing between letters and words.

○ Consider the size and layout of any reading books. In whole-class sessions the pupil will need their own copies of any books.

○ Check writing books for line spacing, line colour, width of lines, size of graph paper, squares in maths books.

○ Enlarge written information, if appropriate.

○ Avoid gloss finishes on paper and books because of problems with glare.

○ Provide short activities and rest breaks for the pupil, if needed.

○ Allow the pupil to use ICT for recording work. Touch-typing might be appropriate.

○ Present information on tape to reduce the time pupils are spending looking at written information.

○ Allow the pupil to record work using a dictaphone.

○ Help the pupil to practise listening skills – children with visual impairments do not have innate compensatory listening skills. Plan listening activities into the curriculum.

○ Use concrete objects and make a point of giving the pupil tactile experiences.

○ Introduce social skills programmes to develop social skills, as the pupil can miss facial expressions and gestures.

Speech and language difficulties: general indicators

Children with specific speech and language difficulties are usually pupils whose development in other areas is generally typical of their age. Children can have difficulties relating to one or a combination of the following areas:

Receptive language

○ Problems relating to understanding.
○ Difficulty following instructions.
○ Attention problems – misunderstanding what has been said.
○ Behaviour and social problems.
○ These often become more noticeable as the language demands of the curriculum increase.

Expressive language

○ Difficulty structuring sentences and in the development of vocabulary.
○ Word-finding difficulties – unable to come up with the right word.
○ Uses incorrect names for things.
○ Problems learning new words.

Pragmatics

○ Odd use of language in social situations.
○ Misunderstands verbal and non-verbal rules.
○ Problems with play and developing friendships.
○ Problems turn-taking.
○ Unusual intonation in the voice.
○ Eye contact – too little or too much.
○ Use of stereotypical or learned phrases often inappropriate to the context.

Speech

○ Problems producing specific sounds, but not those usually associated with normal language development. Many young children experience difficulties with particular sounds.

Children often have associated difficulties with:

o motor skills
o emotional and social behaviour
o attention.

LIST 48

Speech and language difficulties: a checklist

Difficulties with speech and language are often identified preschool. However, some children are not identified until they begin nursery or Reception or older. The following checklist could be a starting point for gathering information.

- ○ Is the pupil learning English as a second language?
- ○ Is the pupil's speech clear or not clear?
- ○ Is the volume appropriate to the context and activity?
- ○ Are there any problems with particular sounds that most other pupils have mastered?
- ○ Is the grammar used appropriate to the pupil's age – tenses, plurals, conjunctions, words missed in sentences, endings missed?
- ○ Does the pupil use question words, such as where, what, who?
- ○ Does the pupil use pronouns?
- ○ What is the pupil's attention span when listening to instructions and stories or during practical activities?
- ○ Does the pupil follow instructions – the first part only, the first and second parts of an instruction, or not at all?
- ○ Does the pupil use and understand concepts relating to time, emotions, location, shape and size?
- ○ Can the pupil classify things into categories?
- ○ Are there limited verbal responses?
- ○ Is the pupil able to sequence ideas into a verbal response?
- ○ Does the pupil engage in play situations with others or solitary/repetitive play?
- ○ Are there problems with social skills, such as turn-taking?

Next steps

- ○ Use more detailed speech and language checklists and assessments to clarify in more detail areas of difficulty. The Speech and Language Therapy Service will usually advise on these.
- ○ Use the P scales as a way of gathering more detailed information (see List 54 P scales).
- ○ Draw up an IEP with SMART targets if appropriate (see List 65 Individual education plans).

- Refer to curriculum guidance for supporting pupils across the curriculum.
- Refer the pupil to the Speech and Language Therapy Service.

Speech and language difficulties: supporting pupils

○ Plan time to liaise with parents, carers and professionals.

○ Make activities visual – use pictures to label and identify equipment.

○ Make the daily timetable visual and prepare the pupil for change.

○ Encourage the pupil to make eye contact – say the pupil's name to gain attention and praise them for responding.

○ Break down information into small and manageable chunks – support with visual cues, such as pictures and diagrams, appropriate to the age of the pupil.

○ Break down tasks and talk them through with the pupil, providing visual prompts.

○ Simplify language – use simple vocabulary and sentence structures.

○ Teach new technical vocabulary through repetition and visual methods, such as mind-maps.

○ Provide the pupil with key topic and vocabulary lists.

○ Check to see if the pupil has understood – look for facial expressions and ask the pupil to say in their own words what he/she has to do.

○ Use concrete apparatus and real-life examples wherever possible – this is often a feature of the curriculum in primary school.

○ Allow the pupil time to respond and provide them with visual supports of pictures and diagrams in order to sequence their responses.

○ Use speaking frames and writing frames across the curriculum to help with vocabulary, grammar and sequencing – the pupil will be supported and encouraged to develop speech and language skills in context.

○ Use alternative recording methods.

○ Cut down on background noise and distractions.

○ Be aware of difficulties that might occur at breaktimes and consider using a buddy system.

○ Provide social skills training.

○ Provide opportunities for the pupil to focus on what they can do well and praise them for it.

○ Provide support in group work if needed – ensure that there are good language models and that the pupil has the social skills to manage group activities as they might feel overwhelmed.

○ Be aware that some pupils might also have literacy difficulties.

Observation and Assessment 5

Why we need assessment

Assessment is an integral part of the teaching and learning process and is especially important for those with additional needs. There are various forms of assessment and whatever form is used will depend on the information to be gathered.

We do assessments to:

o support pupils' learning and identify strengths and weaknesses
o provide feedback to pupils
o assess the effectiveness of a particular teaching method or strategy
o inform future curriculum planning
o provide information to support decision-making
o communicate with and inform parents
o motivate
o maintain standards – both internal and external.

Assessments should be:

o valid – does the assessment measure what it is supposed to do? For example, it should not grade a pupil's handwriting if creative writing and composition are the criteria being assessed.
o reliable – a reliable assessment would produce the same results if it were repeated on individuals or with similar groups of pupils.
o fair – everyone should have an equal chance at the assessment.

Types of assessment

The types of assessment that will inform the provision for pupils with special needs include:

Summative assessment

○ Allows you to assess the effectiveness of SEN interventions and to monitor pupil progress over time. This information is essential for your contribution to the school's self-evaluation form (SEF).

○ Usually takes place at the end of a year, a course, a module or scheme of work.

○ Summarizes attainment at a particular point in time, with reference to objectives and outcomes of the course.

Formative assessment

○ Allows continual monitoring of individual learning – important when working with pupils who tend to learn in very small incremental steps as it helps to identify the next small step that is required. Also, if any learning is 'forgotten' then any such gaps can be identified and filled.

○ Encourages the development of pupils' self-assessment skills.

○ Actively involves pupils in their own learning.

○ Considers how pupils learn.

○ Encourages the development of productive questioning.

○ Provides effective feedback to pupils.

○ Acknowledges emotional and motivational aspects of assessment.

○ Teaching and learning are modified on the basis of assessment evidence.

Criterion-referenced assessment

○ Establishes whether each pupil has achieved a specific skill or grasped certain concepts.

○ Finds out how much the pupil knows before teaching begins and after it is finished.

○ Each individual is compared with that preset standard of achievement rather than with other pupils.

○ Pupil achievement is usually reported in terms of skill achievement.

○ Examples of criterion referenced assessment include the National Curriculum levels.

Norm-referenced assessment

○ Discriminates between high and low achievers.
○ Tests used compare pupils' scores against the scores of a sample population group.
○ Scores are usually expressed in terms of a percentile, a grade, a standard score or stanine.
○ Achievement is usually plotted in terms of broad skill areas, and some report achievement for individual skills.
○ Examples include standardized reading assessments and cognitive assessments.

Ipsative assessment

○ Assessment against a pupil's previous best performance.

Formative assessment

This ongoing classroom-based assessment is particularly effective for monitoring the progress of pupils with special educational needs.

Effective questioning

Formative assessment or assessment for learning includes the use of effective questioning. This helps to assess pupils' understanding and is a useful way of encouraging them and providing feedback.

- Make sure that pupils have time to respond when questions are asked.
- Use open-ended questioning if appropriate – how, what and why.
- Allow pupils to work together to answer questions.
- See incorrect answers as a way of exploring misunderstandings.
- Make sure questions are worth asking.

Marking and giving feedback

- Place the emphasis on the feedback comments and not the grades as these are often interpreted negatively by pupils.
- Make comments directly related to the task – give verbal feedback.
- Comment on what has gone well for the pupil and make suggestions for improvement but keep these to a manageable number and do not simply provide answers and solutions. Feedback should help to build on what has been learnt.
- Discuss suggestions with pupils.

Traffic lighting

This is a useful way of providing feedback to pupils. Use colour codes red, orange and green.

- Green – skill acquired
- Orange – skill developing
- Red – skill needs to be learnt.

○ Encourages pupils to understand what they need to learn and why, and to be involved in assessing their own understanding and identifying future areas for learning.

○ Helps pupils to understand the way in which learning is to be evaluated.

○ Peer assessment helps pupils clarify their own understanding.

○ Pupils can often accept criticisms of work from each other that they might not accept from the teacher.

For further information see www.qca.org.uk or *Inside the Black Box: raising standards through classroom assessment* by Paul Black and Dylan Wiliam (King's College London, 1998, re-issued by NFER Nelson, 2004).

LIST 53 Observation

Observation is a highly appropriate way of collecting information about pupils with special needs as it can be done without their direct involvement. It can be carried out by class teachers or adults who are familiar with pupils without the pressure of an individual formal assessment situation.

You might decide to observe:

○ individual characteristics
○ verbal and non-verbal communication
○ activities
○ skills attainment and performance
○ environment.

Types of observation

○ Unstructured observation
   – not planned
   – allows an observer freedom to record
   – can lack objectivity.
○ Structured observation
   – usually outlines what is to be observed
   – defines how observations will be made, recorded and coded
   – can be recorded in categories where detailed descriptions of behavioural characteristics are devised before observations, or in checklists or rating scales (behaviour is rated on a scale).

Pupil–observer relationship

Observations can be:

○ participant – where the observer and pupil interact during observation
○ overt – the pupil is aware of observation
○ covert – the pupil is not aware of observation
○ non-participant – the observer and pupil do not interact (can be overt or covert).

Time

Data can be collected through:

○ time-sampling – making an observation for a set period of time at pre-determined intervals, e.g. observe two minutes in every ten, or observe for two minutes at six randomly selected times in an hour
○ event-sampling – making an observation every time an event occurs.

P scales

P scales are a method of assessment recommended by the DfES for use with pupils making slower progress or working at the early levels of the National Curriculum. They provide a summative assessment and are used annually and/or at the end of a Key Stage.

The P scales break down the curriculum into eight small steps (P1–8) leading to Level 1 of the National Curriculum. The first three levels, P1–3, are the same for each subject, whereas P4–8 are subject-specific.

They are useful for:

○ demonstrating the achievement of pupils with special educational needs
○ enabling attainment to be measured in more detail
○ enabling relevant targets to be set.

Commercial material that supports the P scales

○ PACE (P Scale Assessment of the National Curriculum from Equals) – www.equals.co.uk.
○ PIVATS (Performance Indicators for Value Added Target Setting) – www.lancashire.gov.uk.
○ B Squared – www.bsquaredsen.co.uk.

More useful information

○ Information on English, mathematics and science can be found in *Supporting the Target Setting Process* (DfES 0065/2001).
○ For information on other subjects see *Planning, teaching and assessing the curriculum for pupils with learning difficulties* (QCA/01/738).

Information gathering and assessment

When you come to target setting and planning for pupils with SEN, class teachers will already have a large amount of information and it is often a case of collecting what is already there. Other information can be gathered through everyday classroom practice, although sometimes specific assessments might be needed. Consider all the following sources of information.

General information

- ○ Early Learning Goals, National Curriculum levels, P scales.
- ○ SATs results.
- ○ Information relating to health, vision and hearing.

Parents' and carers' views

- ○ Relevant information on development.
- ○ What is he/she like at home?
- ○ What do they see as the child's strengths and difficulties?
- ○ What works well at home – with behaviour and learning?

Pupils' views

- ○ Perceptions of learning and behaviour at school.
- ○ What does he/she enjoy or find difficult?
- ○ What helps them most?
- ○ What would they like to improve?

Views of other staff and adults who work with the pupil

- ○ Teaching assistants.
- ○ Volunteers.

Interventions that have been tried

- ○ Differentiation.
- ○ Groupings.
- ○ Additional adult support (teacher, teaching assistant, volunteer).
- ○ Additional literacy or numeracy support programmes.
- ○ Booster classes.
- ○ Changes to the learning environment to facilitate access to the curriculum.

Assessment of strengths as well as concerns

o What does the pupil do well?

o What type of support or activity works best for the pupil?

L I S T 56 Assessing literacy skills

Phonological awareness

This is the ability to recognize and manipulate sounds in words we hear and say. Can the pupil:

○ identify words beginning with the same sound
○ identify and generate rhyming words, using pictures and spoken words
○ understand segmentation – clapping the number of words in a sentence or syllables in a word
○ identify if two words start with same phoneme
○ identify initial, final and medial sounds in words
○ understand phoneme deletion, e.g. taking p from pat leaves at
○ understand phoneme substitution, e.g. replacing the h in hat with p gives pat
○ blend phonemes into vc (vowel consonant) and cvc (consonant vowel consonant) words?

Phonics

This is a pupil's knowledge of letters and sounds. Can the pupil:

○ recite the alphabet
○ understand the names and sounds of upper and lower case printed letters
○ match sounds to symbols
○ write letters from oral dictation?

Reading

Complete a miscue analysis using an appropriate text (see List 85 and 86 on miscue analysis). Observe the behaviour and strategies used when reading. Does the pupil:

○ talk about the text
○ answer literal and inferential questions
○ follow the text to reach conclusions and make predictions
○ follow the print or skip words and lines
○ use phonic, picture and context cues
○ confuse letters
○ read slowly or perhaps quickly but without comprehending

○ understand concepts such as word, letter, title, author, index, chapters, where to start reading?

Analyse reading scores on a standardized reading assessment.

Handwriting

Look at:

○ whether the pupil is right- or left-handed
○ pencil grip
○ letter size and formation
○ orientation of writing
○ legibility.

Spelling

Can the pupil:

○ spell high-frequency words or those from the National Literacy Strategy, and if so, which ones
○ spell simple rimes (using the ends of the words to teach patterns), e.g. at, am, an
○ spell cvc words
○ understand initial and final blends?

Also consider:

○ evidence of omissions, additions, letters in the wrong order, same words spelt differently, and high-frequency words or spelling patterns spelt correctly
○ whether the pupil uses analogy to develop spelling
○ whether spelling reflects phonic knowledge
○ strategies the pupil uses to learn spellings
○ spelling in a standardized test.

Writing

Consider:

○ how writing content compares to oral ability
○ the content, sequencing, use of punctuation, spelling, sentence construction, vocabulary
○ methods used to develop written work
○ alternative methods of recording written work that might have been tried.

LIST 57

Assessing numeracy skills

Pupils will be assessed against National Numeracy Strategy objectives and P levels. Does the pupil have problems with:

- learning number facts and times tables
- sequencing – counting forwards, backwards, days of week, recalling tables, completing tasks in order
- visual perception – recognizing symbols and shapes, etc.
- spatial awareness – working with spatial patterns, three-dimensional figures, recognizing three-dimensional figures in two dimensions
- understanding and using the language of mathematics – problems with specific vocabulary such as triangle, circle, subtraction, and with the meanings of words such as match, order
- short-term memory – limited memory storage causes overload and the pupil forgets a sequence of instructions
- some aspects of mathematics seeming more difficult than others
- recording and presentation of numeracy work?

How does the pupil:

- contribute to oral and mental parts of numeracy sessions
- respond to concrete and visual resources
- approach problem-solving activities?

Also consider:

- what intervention has been tried, how successful this has been and what progress the pupil made
- the pupil's attitudes and feelings about mathematics and numeracy tasks.

Evaluating speech, language and communication

Assessment in speech, language and communication is related to National Curriculum objectives. Does the pupil:

○ appear reluctant to speak in many situations, such as whole class, small groups or on an individual level with an adult? Are there instances when the pupil is more willing or confident to speak (at home, with friends)

○ understand and use non-verbal communication (gestures, tones of voice, facial expressions)

○ make their needs known

○ have difficulty finding words

○ have any difficulty producing particular sounds at the beginning or end of words or consonant clusters

○ listen to class books and stories

○ understand prepositions

○ follow instructions when they are in one, two or three parts

○ follow instructions relating to everyday routines and tasks

○ initiate conversations

○ communicate with peers

○ contribute in class discussions, small group discussions or individually

○ classify information into categories

○ retell, sequence and summarize information?

Also consider:

○ clarity of speech and intelligibility, including volume and intonation

○ attention and concentration

○ grammar – use of conjunctions, determiners, tenses and plurals

○ length of utterances – one word, two words, short phrases

○ vocabulary – is it age appropriate? Use of naming vocabulary, pronouns, adverbs, comparatives

○ play skills – does the pupil play with others or alone

○ is English the pupil's first language?

Observing behaviour

Collect information on the pupil's:

○ response to the school behaviour policy
○ response to positive classroom management strategies – rules and routines
○ frequency, nature and duration of poor behaviour
○ behaviour in different lessons
○ behaviour with other pupils in class and at breaktimes
○ social skills – is the pupil willing to take turns, share, listen to the views of others and generally participate in interactions
○ curriculum attainments
○ ABC record (antecedent, behaviour and consequences) – this can be useful for providing detailed information about a pupil's behaviour
○ friendship patterns
○ speech and language abilities
○ self-esteem
○ general health
○ family circumstances.

Also consider:

○ contact and liaison with parents – listen to the parents' views of the child's behaviour, social skills and emotional functioning
○ what the pupil is like with different adults – other curriculum teachers, teaching assistants, volunteers, lunchtime supervisors
○ what activities the pupil enjoys or really dislikes
○ whether the pupil could be the victim of bullying or even the bully
○ interventions tried above and beyond those generally recommended in whole-school rewards and sanctions, and responses to interventions – find out what worked and what has not been so successful.

LIST 60   Checking motor skills

Collect information on the following areas of a pupil's motor skills, either through observation in PE, the playground, classroom or through some individual activity sessions:

○ balance
○ posture
○ ball skills – throwing and catching skills, kicking, dribbling, use of bats and rackets
○ movement – walking and running, changing directions. Note arm movements when carrying out these activities
○ pencil grip
○ letter formation and handwriting
○ cutting skills
○ speed and rate of work.

Can the pupil:

○ pedal a tricycle or ride a bicycle
○ complete threading activities
○ use a knife and fork
○ dress and undress
○ manage buttons and zips
○ tie shoelaces?

Also take note of any interventions already tried, such as activities to develop hand–eye coordination, or handwriting programmes.

L I S T 61 Wechsler Intelligence Scale for Children

Commonly used assessments of cognitive functioning include the Wechsler Intelligence Scale for Children, third edition, UK (WISC III – UK) and fourth edition, UK (WISC – IV UK). The fourth edition is the most recent, revised version.

These scales contain a range of sub-tests that can be administered to a pupil. Each of these tests attempts to investigate different areas of ability. The sub-tests are then put together in different combinations to produce scores which can be analysed by education professionals.

While WISCIII and IV vary slightly, you may come across the following index scores:

○ Verbal Comprehension Index – a measure of verbal abilities.
○ Perceptual Reasoning Index – a measure of visual processing abilities.
○ Freedom from Distractibility Index – a measure of ability not to become distracted.
○ Processing Speed Index – a measure of how quickly visual symbols are processed.
○ Working Memory Index – a measure of auditory memory.
○ Verbal Intelligence Quotient – a broader measure of verbal abilities.
○ Performance IQ – a broader measure of visual, manual and perceptual abilities.
○ Full Scale IQ – an amalgamation of everything!

Scores in both tests include:

○ Raw score – this represents the number of correct responses or score gained on an individual sub-test.
○ Scaled score – sub-test raw scores are converted to an age-related scaled score. These range between 1 and 19, with 1 the lowest and 19 the highest. A scaled score of 10 represents the average performance for a particular age group. Scaled scores are standard scores.
○ Composite score – these are standard scores based on the sums of scaled scores. Sums of scaled scores are converted to a composite

score where 100 is the average performance of pupils of a similar age. About 58% of children score between 85 and 115.

○ Percentile ranks – these indicate where a pupil's score lies in relation to other pupils. Percentile ranks usually range from 1–99, with 50 as the mean and median. A percentile rank of 25 means that a pupil scored better than 25% of pupils and 75% scored as well or better.

Legislation and Government Initiatives 6

SEN Code of Practice

All SENCOs need to be familiar with the SEN Code of Practice and all schools will have a copy of this. Further information can be found in the SEN Toolkit produced by the DfES – a purple box that you should be able to find in your school.

Since 2002 schools have been required to follow the revised Code of Practice which is linked to the Disability Act 2001. The revised Code stresses that:

- all teachers are teachers of special educational needs
- the special educational needs of children will normally be met in mainstream settings
- SEN provision is an integral part of the school development plan
- children with SEN should be offered full access to a broad curriculum
- parents should be treated as partners
- pupils should be consulted and their views taken into account
- LEAs must arrange for pupils with SEN to be provided with a service giving advice and information
- there should be a graduated approach to meeting special educational needs.

England, Scotland, Northern Ireland and Wales have slightly different legislation. It is especially important to note that Scotland no longer uses the term special needs but has a broader category of 'additional needs'. This information refers to the English legislation.

School Action

When a class teacher identifies that a pupil has SEN they devise strategies that are additional to or different from those provided as part of the school's usual differentiated curriculum. The class teacher remains responsible for working with the child on a daily basis and for planning an individualized programme and drawing up an individual education plan (IEP). The parents are consulted and involved in this process.

The SENCO could take the lead in:

○ planning future interventions for the pupil in discussion with colleagues
○ monitoring and reviewing the action.

Triggers for School Action

The pupil will be placed in School Action if they have the following difficulties:

○ Makes little or no progress, even when teaching approaches are targeted.
○ Shows signs of difficulty in developing literacy or mathematics skills which result in poor attainment in some curriculum areas.
○ Presents persistent emotional and behavioural difficulties which are not improved by behaviour management.
○ Has sensory or physical problems and continues to make little or no progress, despite the provision of specialist equipment.
○ Has communication and/or interaction difficulties and continues to make little or no progress, despite the provision of specialist equipment.

School Action Plus

The pupil will be placed in School Action Plus if the SENCO and class teacher, in consultation with the parents, ask for help from external services. Then:

○ advice or support is provided from outside specialists
○ additional or different strategies to those at School Action are put in place, e.g. a more individualized literacy programme.

L I S T 64   Statutory assessment and statements

Comprehensive information on procedures for statementing can be found in Chapter 7 and Chapter 8 of the SEN Code of Practice and in the SEN Toolkit. Chapter 9 explains the process for annual reviews. Your local authority will also have detailed information. The statement will include:

○ a description of the pupil's current difficulties
○ a statement of the pupil's special needs
○ the provision to be made by the local authority and the school (including access to teaching assistants)
○ appropriate facilities and equipment required
○ modifications to the curriculum required
○ the actual placement of the pupil
○ any non-educational needs, e.g. access to a physiotherapist, occupational therapist and speech and language therapist.

Attached to the statement should be all the advice collected by the local authority.

Individual education plans

A pupil will have an individual education plan (IEP) if they:

o are placed in Early Years Action or Early Years Action Plus
o are placed in School Action or School Action Plus
o have a statement of SEN.

If a provision map is in place and the targets are apparent in a teacher's planning, an IEP may not be required.

Group education plans can be used if:

o there are several pupils working on the same target
o each pupil is individually reviewed against the targets.

What should be included on an IEP?

o Short-term targets which should be SMART (Specific, Measurable, Achievable, Relevant, Time-related). There are occasions when less measurable but assessable targets that can record progress are more appropriate.
o Teaching strategies to be used.
o Provision.
o Review date.
o Success or exit criteria.

Monitoring and reviewing IEPs

o Keep under continual review.
o Evaluate at least twice a year (parents' evenings can be used as one of the review dates).
o Review the pupil's needs, previous targets and strategies and set new ones. Establish new success criteria.
o Involve the parents and the pupil in the process.

A pupil profile (individual management profile) should accompany an IEP or provision map. This should include:

o baseline assessment
o the pupil's particular needs
o general strategies to enable access and optimum learning conditions
o the pupil's strengths
o long-term aims to put the IEP in context.

Provision maps

Provision mapping is the means of documenting the range of support and resources available to pupils with SEN within a school. It enables schools to show how the SEN budget has been spent, including resources and staffing, along with time costs. It allows SENCOs to look at provision within and between years to make sure all needs are catered for and there is little duplication.

Provision maps are used to:

o demonstrate how SEN support is deployed across the school
o form the basis for writing IEPs
o provide evidence for the use of resources when talking to governors, parents and other parties, such as the LEA
o audit how well provision matches need, and recognize gaps in provision
o cost provision accurately
o assess school effectiveness when linked with improving outcomes for pupils
o focus attention on whole-school issues of teaching and learning, rather than on individual pupil issues
o record changes in provision and help pupils to transfer easily from class to class or school to school.

Types of provision mapping

When drawing up a provision map, the following need to be considered:

o who to involve
o what information is needed
o what to include
o how it will be put into practice
o how the provision will be monitored and reviewed
o how evaluations will be used to inform future practice.

Maps can detail the additional provision in a variety of ways.

o By year group or Key Stage or, if the classes include two years, even by class.
o Linked to the three Waves (see List 77 The three Waves). This could include SEN provision and also the provision made as part of quality-first teaching (where the learning environment is made as inclusive as possible).
o Within the four areas of difficulty identified in the Code of Practice:
  – cognition and learning
  – communication and interaction
  – emotional, behavioural and social
  – sensory and physical.
o According to areas of disability, e.g. ASD, ADHD, specific learning difficulties, etc.

There are many examples of provision maps on the Internet and also in DfES documents. A good place to start looking is your local authority website.

Drawing up your provision map

It is not essential to cost your provision map – different interventions can just be identified. If you do calculate the costs, however, you will be able to show the most cost-effective provision and it will be clearer to any interested parties how the SEN budget has been spent.

Only provision which is 'additional to and different from' what is available for all pupils should be included on an SEN provision map.

- ○ Identify the amount of money in the budget earmarked for SEN.
- ○ Have information on identified needs within the school available.
- ○ Use the chosen template to brainstorm all the provision.
- ○ Check it against individual pupils' needs to make sure nothing is omitted.
- ○ Calculate pupil–staff ratios for each type of provision.
- ○ Identify staff involved, e.g. teacher, TA, learning mentor, etc.
- ○ Calculate the average weekly cost in time.
- ○ Calculate the annual cost (x 38 weeks).
- ○ List general provision which cannot be tracked to individual pupils but which benefits all pupils with SEN, e.g. admin time, continuing professional development and general resources.
- ○ Cost general provision.
- ○ Compare 'actual cost' with SEN budget.

The SENCO is likely to be a key person in monitoring the school's response to the Act.

Main points about the Act

○ It is unlawful for every type of school, including independent ones, in England and Wales to discriminate against pupils with a learning disability.

○ A pupil has a disability if they have 'a physical or mental impairment, which has a substantial and long-term effect on a person's ability to carry out normal day-to-day activities'.

○ The majority of disabled children will also have a special educational need. This is defined as pupils who have any difficulty in accessing education and need any special educational provision to be made for them.

○ Schools must not treat disabled pupils less favourably than other pupils and must make reasonable adjustments. (Guidance on this is given in Chapters 5 and 6 of the Code of Practice.)

○ If a parent considers that a school has discriminated against their child they can make a claim of unlawful discrimination. Normally this is done through the Special Educational Needs Tribunal (SENDIST) (see List 76 SEN tribunals).

○ Schools are required to have a regularly reviewed accessibility plan. This should state how the school intends to make:
  – improvements in access to the curriculum
  – physical improvements to increase access to the buildings and teaching areas
  – improvements in the provision of information in various formats for disabled pupils and their parents.

(For more detailed information have a look at the Code of Practice for Schools available from the Disability Rights Commission www.drc-gb.org.)

LIST 70   Every Child Matters

Every Child Matters: Change for Children is a government document setting out a new approach to the well-being of children and young people from birth to the age of 19. It gives a commitment to improving provision for children with SEN. Its implementation will be part of the wider developments stemming from the Every Child Matters agenda and the Children's National Service Framework.

The rights of children are divided into five areas. All children have a right to:

Stay safe

- Be safe from maltreatment, neglect, violence and sexual exploitation.
- Be safe from accidental injury and death.
- Be safe from bullying and discrimination.
- Be safe from crime and anti-social behaviour in and out of school.
- Have security, stability and be cared for.

Be healthy

- Be physically healthy.
- Be mentally and emotionally healthy.
- Be sexually healthy.
- Lead a healthy lifestyle.
- Choose not to take illegal drugs.

Enjoy and achieve

- Be ready for school.
- Attend and enjoy school.
- Achieve stretching national educational standards at primary school.
- Achieve personal and social development and enjoy recreation.
- Achieve stretching national educational standards at secondary school.

Have economic well-being

○ Engage in further education, employment or training on leaving school.
○ Be ready for employment.
○ Live in decent homes and sustainable communities.
○ Have access to transport and material goods.
○ Live in households free from low income.

Make a positive contribution

○ Engage in decision-making and support the community and the environment.
○ Engage in law-abiding and positive behaviour in and out of school.
○ Develop positive relationships and choose not to bully or discriminate.
○ Develop self-confidence and successfully deal with significant life changes and challenges.
○ Develop enterprising behaviour.

For more detailed information visit the website: www.everychildmatters.gov.uk.

Making Every Child Matters work

The aims of the programme

- Build services around young people.
- Support parents and carers.
- Develop the education workforce, changing culture and practice, and integrate them.
- Provide universal and targeted services across the range 0–19.

The Children Act 2004 provides the legislation to back up the Every Child Matters programme. It details that:

- a children's commissioner is to be appointed
- all services have a duty to cooperate – this will be facilitated by the establishing of children's trusts
- all services have a duty to safeguard and promote the welfare of children
- a database is to be set up to share information. There will be a common assessment framework. Transitions will be supported
- common core skills have been identified for all who work with children
- there will be a single children and young people's plan
- there will be a children's commissioner in every authority
- there will be a joint inspection framework and joint area reviews
- there is a duty to promote the educational achievement of looked-after children.

Ofsted and SEN

In the new Ofsted inspections, self-evaluation is going to be very important. The SENCO is likely to be the person who will take the lead role in evaluating the SEN provision in the school.

General principles

❍ SEN is part of the wider inclusion agenda.
❍ Prominence will be given in inspections to evaluating a school's contribution in promoting the five outcomes with which the Every Child Matters agenda is concerned (See List 70 Every Child Matters).
❍ The inspection will rely heavily on the school's own self-evaluation and planning.
❍ Inspections will take place every three years and will use about a quarter of the current allocation of inspector days.
❍ The number of interviews will be radically reduced and not every teacher will be seen in secondary schools.
❍ Inspection will be regarded as a routine which complements the school's own self-evaluation and reporting. A self-evaluation form (SEF) is written by the school and lodged on Ofsted's website.

When the inspectors arrive. . .

In addition to talking with the pupils, SENCO and a range of support staff, the inspectors may ask to see some written evidence:

○ pupil statements and records – named pupils from vulnerable groups
○ lesson observations, both in the classroom and when the pupil is withdrawn for specific support
○ workbooks
○ data on SEN pupils – overall school and individual pupil level
○ SENCO records, class or subject teacher records and planning, TA records and planning
○ data on lengths of stay at school, mobility, etc.
○ possible case studies – this may include talking to pupils, shadowing in lessons, scrutinizing work, records and progress data
○ pupil diaries or work planners.

They will be looking for, among other things:

○ good teaching practice
○ quality of leadership and management of school at all levels
○ support, care and guidance from the LEA
○ links with parents and other providers
○ attainment and progress of the pupils – both overall and in relation to those with SEN
○ recognition of the school's particular context
○ the commitment of the school to inclusion
○ the whole-school approach to SEN.

They will check:

○ attainment on entry
○ quality of teaching
○ ethos, shared and celebrated throughout the school
○ record-keeping, collection of data – over time and day-to-day
○ targets – are they SMART? Are pupils involved?
○ Every Child Matters issues – are procedures and systems in place?

Ofsted will not look at every aspect of a school but will focus on certain areas. The areas chosen will be decided after scrutinizing:

- Performance and Assessment reports (PANDA), particularly looking at the context of trends, predicted trends and special circumstances
- end of Key Stage National Curriculum results – trends over time, how the results relate to specific cohorts, how targets are set for improvement
- level progress data and transition matrices (progress over time for pupils of all abilities, some comparisons with national averages)
  - progress of those not achieving at National Curriculum Level 1 or n, b, d at the previous Key Stage (n – not awarded a test level; b – working below the level of the test; d – working at the level of the tests but unable to access them)
  - progress of those not quite making a level gain
  - level of SEN within cohort
- school-based progress measures – how these are used to track individuals and set targets
- individual records – how progress is measured and how data is used.

What the inspectors want to see

Ofsted will be looking for evidence of effective teaching of SEN pupils. This will be shown by:

- good in-class support
- early identification of needs
- building on skills through effective and appropriate withdrawal
- careful differentiation by input, through questioning, targeted support, etc.
- phased inclusion, re-integration to support success
- effective planning – with pupils' needs in mind – for the next stage of learning
- continual monitoring of progress
- clarity of learning objectives
- consistency of approach – normal class routines
- recognizing and working to individual strengths and weaknesses
- pace and variety, and teaching to learning styles
- promoting access – overcoming barriers
- positive relationships
- modification of resources
- high expectations
- accurate observation, assessment and consistent recording
- feedback to all necessary parties
- use of other adults
- application, consolidation and generalisation of skills
- use of technology
- dialogue and communication between staff – teamwork
- different ways of explaining tasks – prompting, rehearsing, key words, key visuals
- promoting independence
- positioning of pupils.

Judging effective leadership

In order to judge how effectively the school is led and managed, Ofsted will look at:

- how leaders and managers at all levels set clear direction leading to improvements in standards, support, personal development, the quality of care and, where relevant, any extended services
- how the school and services are managed and performance is monitored and quality assured
- how governors meet their statutory responsibilities (including the SEN governor)
- how well equality of opportunity is promoted and discrimination tackled so that all learners make good progress
- how efficiently resources are deployed to achieve value for money
- the adequacy of staffing and accommodation and how effectively they are deployed
- how well leaders promote the integration of care, education and any extended services to enliven and enhance learning
- the effectiveness of the links made with other providers of education and care.

SEN tribunals

As a SENCO it is possible that you might be asked to attend a tribunal. For example, the local authority may have refused to formally assess one of your pupils, or there may be dispute about the provision. You could be a witness for either the parent or the local authority.

If a parent speaks to you about the possibility that their child is being discriminated against it is useful to inform them that before they resort to a tribunal they could discuss their anxieties with the Parent Partnership or go to disagreement resolution. Your local authority will be able to give you the appropriate contact numbers.

The format of the tribunal is clearly laid out on the SENDIST (Special Educational Needs and Disability Tribunal) website at www.sendist.gov.uk.

Timescale for a tribunal

- ○ local authority makes a decision – refuses an assessment; finalizes a statement; amends a statement; ceases to maintain statement.
- ○ Parents are informed of their right to appeal (two-month deadline).
- ○ Parents send in notice of appeal to SENDIST. At this stage the parents must decide on the grounds for appeal and start to think about evidence and witnesses.
- ○ SENDIST registers the appeal and sends copies of the notice of appeal to the local authority.
- ○ Parents and the local authority have 30 working days to make a case statement and provide evidence. A tribunal date will be arranged during this period.
- ○ The hearing takes place.
- ○ SENDIST sends the decision to parents and the local authority within ten working days.
- ○ If the parents lose the tribunal, the local authority's initial decision stands.
- ○ If the parents win the tribunal, the new decision can be implemented.
- ○ Parents or the local authority ask for a review of the decision within ten days and/or appeal to a judicial review within 28 days.

If you are going to a tribunal it is helpful to discuss issues with your local authority SEN team who will be able to give you advice and support.

Special Interventions   **7**

LIST 77   The three Waves

In 2002 the Government produced a publication as part of the Primary Strategy called *Including all children in the literacy hour and daily mathematical lesson* (DfES 0465/2002). This suggested that support for pupils could be provided in three 'Waves'.

- ○ Wave 1 – the effective inclusion of all pupils using quality-first teaching (i.e. teaching that attempts to remove all barriers to learning).
- ○ Wave 2 – small-group, low-cost intervention, e.g. booster classes, Springboard programmes, early literacy support (ELS) programmes, for children who can be expected to 'catch up' with their peers as a result of the intervention.
- ○ Wave 3 – specific, targeted intervention for pupils requiring SEN support.

An example of the types of support that should be provided at Wave 1 (quality-first teaching) includes the following:

Foundation stage

- ○ Planned opportunities for communication and language for thinking through talk or signing.
- ○ Planned opportunities for singing and saying rhymes and songs, including those which are number related.
- ○ Use of big books and posters to develop text and number-related activities.
- ○ Participation in parental involvement initiatives related to literacy and mathematics.
- ○ Introduction to a range of simple shapes to identify their properties and names.
- ○ Development of phonological awareness.
- ○ Support from a teaching assistant for small groups of pupils in

planned or child-initiated activities or for targeted pupils during whole-class sessions.

Key Stages 1 and 2

○ Differentiated activities which enable the pupils to work independently.
○ Focused group work with the teacher.
○ Opportunities taken to model activities for independent work or further reinforcement by a teaching assistant.
○ Support from a teaching assistant for targeted pupils during whole-class sessions.
○ Provision of independent activities which ensure a range of opportunities to encourage discussion and cooperation between pupils.
○ Provision of independent activities which ensure a range of opportunities for recording, and alternatives to pencil and paper tasks.
○ Effective use of the plenary to assess, secure and reinforce the learning of all pupils.
○ Access strategies planned and utilized to include all pupils in daily literacy hour and mathematics lessons.

Further examples can be found in the DfES publication, as well as examples of support at Waves 2 and 3.

Literacy intervention

Here are some suggested interventions for pupil's with literacy
difficulties, including dyslexia (see Lists 35–41 on dyslexia).

Wave 1

❍ Participation in the literacy hour is a minimum requirement. The
   provision should be differentiated adequately and this could be
   supplemented by help at home with reading.
❍ Quality teaching must be provided.
❍ Pupils might even receive in-class support for some activities.

Wave 2

For pupils performing below average but who might be expected to
catch up with their peers. The DfES has produced materials to
support interventions. These include:

❍ Early Literacy Strategy (ELS) for Year 1
❍ Additional Literacy Support (ALS) for Year 3
❍ Further Literacy Support (FLS) for Year 5
❍ booster classes and summer school for Year 7
❍ Literacy Progress Units (secondary-age pupils).

Wave 3

Targeted approaches for pupils on School Action, School Action
Plus or those with a statement of SEN. The DfES has produced a
list of (apparently) effective, commercial packages:

❍ AcceleRead/AccelerWrite (Years 3–6)
❍ Better Reading Partnerships (Years 1–6)
❍ The Catch Up Project (Years 2–6)
❍ Cued Spelling (all ages)
❍ Family Literacy (Reception, Years 1,2 and 4)
❍ Interactive Assessment and Teaching (IAT) (Years 2 and 3)
❍ Multi-sensory Teaching System for Reading (MTSR) (Years 2–
   6)
❍ Paired Reading (Years 1–6)
❍ Paired Writing (Reception–Year 6)
❍ Phono graphix (Key Stages 1–4)

- Reading Intervention/Sound Linkage (Years 1–6)
- Reading Recovery (Years 1 and 2)
- Reciprocal Teaching (Key Stages 1–4)
- RITA (Years 2–3)
- THRASS (Years 2–6).

For further information go to www.standards.dfes.gov.uk/primary publications/literacy and see *Targeting support: choosing and implementing interventions for children with significant literacy difficulties* (DfES 0201/2003).

Difficulties with mathematics

Many pupils experience difficulties developing mathematical skills, and others develop some skills but have gaps in their knowledge and understanding of certain areas. You might find pupils experience difficulties with:

- understanding and using specific mathematical vocabulary, such as terms relating to shape and space, length, mass and capacity
- basic number operations (adding, subtracting, calculating more than or less than, dividing, multiplying)
- learning, retaining and recalling basic number facts. This makes it very difficult to move to more advanced calculations. Often pupils continue to rely on practical apparatus, such as counters and cubes, for 'working out' sums
- recognizing numbers and symbols easily (%, −, +, =)
- sequencing – counting forwards and backwards and ordering numbers, recalling days of week, months of year
- spatial awareness, such as recognizing and copying patterns, symmetry, naming and recognizing two-dimensional and three-dimensional shapes, recognizing shapes in different orientations
- following directions
- recording mathematical calculations using set procedures
- remembering instructions and being able to manipulate information to work out mental mathematical problems
- recording information and using equipment – particularly if the pupil has fine motor and gross motor difficulties.

Many children and adults can also become anxious about mathematical tasks and find it difficult even to attempt them. Pupils with the following areas of need can experience particular problems developing mathematical skills:

- learning difficulties
- sensory impairment
- Down syndrome
- specific learning difficulties, such as dyslexia and dyspraxia.

Based on *Specific Learning Difficulties in Mathematics: A Classroom Approach* by O. El-Naggar (NASEN, 1996).

L I S T 80   Intervention for pupils with mathematical difficulties

The National Numeracy Strategy has intervention based on three levels.

Wave 1

○ Provision includes the effective inclusion of all pupils in a daily, high-quality numeracy hour.

Wave 2

○ Provision for pupils who are performing below average but who might be expected to catch up. This includes the Springboard programme for Years 3–7.
○ Time-limited provision in the form of small-group intervention to accelerate progress.

Wave 3

○ Additional time-limited provision to enhance progress where Waves 1 and 2 on their own are not sufficient.
○ Provision of focused teaching to tackle fundamental errors and misconceptions that are preventing progress.
○ Based on an assessment for learning approach.

Don't forget the basics

○ Encourage pupils to take risks and have a go.
○ Use easy numbers when introducing new procedures so that the focus is on the method.
○ Go back to what the pupil understands and facts they are secure with before moving on – revisit familiar areas many times.
○ Help pupils rephrase questions to support understanding.
○ Demonstrate using concrete examples.
○ Be aware of the pupil's individual learning style – is he/she the inchworm who adopts a step-by-step approach or the grasshopper who makes intuitive leaps?
○ Check and mark work so that mistakes can be corrected before the pupil forgets the task. Do not highlight too many mistakes as this can contribute to anxiety. Mark and provide feedback using an assessment for learning approach.

DARTs or Direct Activities Related to Texts are ways of extending interaction and developing understanding of text. DARTs can:

○ be used in any subject area
○ make text more manageable to read
○ enable pupils to develop skills such as skimming, scanning and reading text
○ encourage pupils to think about what they are reading
○ encourage discussion
○ help teachers to check pupils' understanding.

Most of the activities below can be used individually or in pairs or small groups to encourage cooperative working. Activities can also be differentiated for pupils working at a variety of levels.

Reconstructing text

○ Text completion – delete words and phrases from a text (cloze procedure). Pupils can then replace them using a set of available words or suggest their own ideas for words. Text completion can be used to focus on key words for reading, spelling, and meaning and also to gain information from the text. An example could be missing out all the conjunctions, pronouns or adjectives.
○ Diagram completion – pupils use information gleaned from the text to label a diagram.
○ Prediction – cut the text into sections and ask pupils to predict what comes next.
○ Sentence stems – pupils complete sentences using information from the text.
○ Sequencing – pupils re-order sections of the text into a logical sequence.
○ Table completion – pupils complete a table with information from the text under particular headings.

Analysing text

○ Diagram and picture construction – pupils use descriptive information from the text to draw a diagram or picture.

- Questions – ask pupils to think of questions about the text for other pupils to answer.
- Text marking – pupils find and underline sections of text, for example, questions or words that relate to a specific topic or begin with a particular letter.
- Summarizing information verbally – can be recorded or put into note form or mind-maps.
- Table construction – pupils use text to construct tables.
- Labelling – pupils label sections of the text.
- Listing information in order of importance.

Paired reading

Paired reading is a method that helps children practise their reading. It takes about 10–20 minutes a day and can be done with a teacher, teaching assistant, helper, family member or carer.

○ The pupil chooses a book. Even if the book might seem too hard or too easy, it can always be changed. After a while the pupil will find out which books they can manage best.

○ Choose a time when the pupil does not prefer to do something else, such as go to a favourite art lesson.

○ Give praise and encouragement and don't make critical comments.

○ Read with the pupil and, if necessary, alter your own speed to make it as fast or slow as the child's.

○ Correct errors by giving the correct word and then join in reading again.

○ When the pupil feels that they are able to read independently, get them to indicate, for example by knocking on the table. Stop reading and, as the pupil reads, provide praise. If the pupil is not able to read a word in about four attempts, continue reading together until they knock again.

○ If the pupil struggles over a word and then succeeds, give praise. If they struggle and then make an error, give the correct word and join in again. If the pupil cannot attempt a word, read it for them. Don't make a big fuss about mistakes, or make them sound out the word, just tell them what the word is and ask the pupil to repeat it after you and then continue reading.

○ Record which books the pupil is reading and note any comments.

○ Remember, the role of the reading partner is to collect information and offer encouragement and support to the reader.

Mind-maps

A mind-map is a visual way of presenting information to aid memory and moves from a linear approach to note-taking. They are useful for pupils and teachers as they enable large amounts of information to be condensed into a simple visual format.

Mind-mapping is useful for:

○ problem-solving
○ planning
○ revision
○ note-taking.

To create a mind-map:

○ start with a blank sheet of paper on which you draw a picture of the topic you are trying to learn about in the centre
○ draw up to nine tapering lines representing themes or words radiating out from the central image
○ off these lines, draw another series of lines, each representing an associated idea. Use colours, symbols and arrows to link associated ideas.

Make sure you:

○ have a coloured picture or image at the centre
○ incorporate images
○ print words
○ put printed words on lines connected to other lines
○ use one word per line
○ use colours throughout.

Spelling tips for pupils

Spelling uses several senses:

- sight – we see the word
- hearing – we listen to the word
- touch – we move our hands as we write the word.

Get pupils to follow this suggested strategy for spelling new or difficult words:

- read the word and say it
- copy the word in larger letters
- look at the word and underline any difficult syllables
- write the word several times with a finger or a pen, saying each part of the word
- check that the word is written correctly.

Spelling rules

Many words can be taught using spelling rules. Use these with your pupils:

- Remember this rhyme to decide if a word should be spelled with ie or ei.

Put i before e (mischief, brief), except after c (received, conceited), or when it sounds like 'a' (neighbour weigh, sleigh).

Remember, there are always exceptions (neither, foreign leisure).

- Some words are particularly troublesome:
  - for irregular plural formations of nouns (nouns that end in a consonant plus y), change y to i and add es (baby/babies, spy/ spies, poppy/poppies).
  - the letter q is always written with u and we say 'kw'. The letter u is not a vowel here (quiet).

Mnemonics

These are rhymes or phrases that help people to remember a particular spelling rule or a word that is particularly difficult to spell. Pupils often enjoy making these up.

- O u lucky duck (ould) – could would should
- I go home today (ight) – fight, sight might
- A rat in the house might eat ice cream (arithmetic)
- Never eat cake eat salmon sandwiches and remain young (necessary)

Analogy

- Use a key word to help spell several words, e.g. air as a key word for pair, chair.
- Don't forget to monitor spelling rules, e.g. share would not apply.

What is miscue analysis?

Miscue analysis involves analysing errors and how a reader comprehends text. This enables teachers to gather information about reading skills so that strategies based on the cues a reader uses can be implemented.

Good readers are those who:

○ read to construct meaning from texts, not just identify words
○ predict or think ahead as they read
○ monitor comprehension and notice if something does not make sense
○ try to solve the problem when something does not make sense or sound grammatically correct.

Miscue analysis is:

○ usually carried out on a text of 100 words
○ can be used with a text with which a pupil is familiar and therefore it is often less stressful for the pupil
○ diagnostic and formative, therefore provides useful information about what to do next
○ administered by teachers, teaching assistants and volunteers.

You will need:

○ an extract of text
○ a record sheet with the text and a place to mark miscues
○ a tape recorder, if required.

When choosing a text:

○ if the pupil can read 95% or more, the text is suitable
○ if the pupil is able to read 90–5%, the pupil will need some support and this might be a better level for guided reading
○ if the pupil can read less than 90%, the text is too difficult so choose a different one.

LIST 86 — Using miscue analysis

- ○ Ask the pupil to read the text aloud in their own time.
- ○ As the pupil reads, mark errors on a photocopied sheet – use the system below.
- ○ If the pupil cannot read a word or hesitates too long, give them the word and mark the record sheet.
- ○ If the pupil continuously pauses and cannot extract any meaning from the text, it is too difficult.

Type of miscue	Explanation	Mark on record sheet
Refusal	Pupil does not read a word	-
Self-correction	Pupil reads incorrectly then corrects	Write 'error' and sc above word
Omission	Pupil misses out a word	Circle the word
Insertion	Pupil adds word/s	∧
Hesitation	Pupil clearly hesitates when decoding a word	H or /
Reversal	Word reversed, e.g. saw/ was	s on its side
Substitution	Incorrect word substituted for word in passage	Cross out and write 'substitute'

Analysing miscues

- ○ Did the pupil preserve the meaning?
- ○ What kind of miscues did the pupil make?
- ○ Does the substituted word make sense in the passage? No – does the pupil focus on decoding, so losing the meaning or does the pupil not focus enough on reading for meaning? Use paired reading, guided reading or DARTs (see List 81 DARTs).
- ○ Does the substituted word make sense in the sentence? No – the pupil has not learned that sentence structure limits possible responses. Use cloze procedure and prediction or DARTS.
- ○ Does the substituted word look and sound like the original? No – decoding letter/sound correspondences are not consolidated.

Managing Teaching Assistants

8

LIST 87   The TA's role: levels 1 and 2

The SENCO is most likely to be the person who line-manages teaching assistants (TAs). To be an effective manager it is therefore important to understand their role. This (and List 88) gives a brief description of the conditions under which TAs could work and the tasks that might be done, and could form the basis of a job description.

Level 1

○ Works under direction and instruction.
○ Requires direct supervision and should not be left alone with a class.
○ Training: DfES induction training.

Tasks:

○ welfare, personal care
○ taking small groups or one-to-one sessions
○ general clerical and organizational support for the teacher
○ preparation, routine maintenance, and operation of materials and equipment.

Level 2

○ Works under the instruction and guidance of the teacher.
○ As a member of the support staff, gains experience, develops new skills or acquires additional qualifications. The role they undertake may need to be reviewed, together with the system of supervision required.
○ Training: NVQ Level 2 for Teaching Assistants.

Tasks:

- welfare, personal support – SEN
- delivering pre-determined learning, care and support programmes
- implementing literacy and numeracy programmes
- assisting with planning cycle
- clerical/administrative support for the teacher and department
- preparation and maintenance of resources
- routine invigilation and marking.

The TA's role: levels 3 and 4

Level 3 and 4 teaching assistants still work under the guidance of a teacher but they should be able to work more independently.

Level 3

○ Works under guidance.
○ The nature of the supervision may vary according to the level of specified work undertaken.
○ Training: NVQ Level 3 for Teaching Assistants.

Tasks:

○ involved in whole planning cycle
○ implementing work programmes
○ evaluation and record-keeping
○ cover supervisor
○ specialist SEN, subject and other support
○ preparation and maintenance of resources and equipment
○ implementing specific work programmes, including assessment
○ providing advice, information, training and supervision for other staff.

Level 4

○ Works under an agreed system of supervision and management.
○ Experienced support staff with appropriate training and qualifications may be given greater autonomy within the framework set by the teacher.
○ Training: must meet the HLTA standards.

Tasks:

○ leading planning cycle, under supervision
○ delivering lessons to groups and whole class
○ managing other staff
○ pastoral support
○ mentoring and counselling
○ management of budget and resources
○ supporting special projects

○ advising teaching staff on a specialist area, equipment and resources.

More information can be found on the website www.lg-employers.gov.uk/publications/index.html under the heading 'School Support Staff – The Way Forward'.

Keeping TAs happy

If TAs are to feel valued and become successful members of the SEN team, the SENCO needs to ensure that they:

- have a good job description which is regularly reviewed
- have a comprehensive induction programme
- have opportunities for relevant training and professional development
- are encouraged to keep a professional portfolio
- are treated as an integral member of the school team
- have an appraisal system to discuss career progression and training opportunities
- have time for planning and evaluation with the teacher
- have time to make resources
- are included in the evaluation of IEPs and SEN interventions
- are included in pupil record-keeping.

What to look for in a TA

The TA's job is very varied but there are some general attributes that the SENCO needs to look for when recruiting staff.

○ Sensitivity
○ Commitment
○ Professionalism and respect for the teaching profession
○ Humour, enthusiasm, interest and love of the job
○ High standards and high expectations of self and others
○ Ability to use initiative and take responsibility in the class
○ Willingness to ask for support when needed
○ Willingness to develop expertise
○ Ability to keep confidences
○ Ability to multi-task and be constantly mobile
○ Ability to control or manage behaviour through non-verbal gestures.

Interpersonal skills

○ Good relationships with adults and pupils
○ Ability to relate to a pupil's needs
○ Ability to share and cooperate with other adults
○ Ability to listen
○ Friendliness and openness
○ Respect for adults and pupils
○ Ability to build and support self-confidence and self-esteem
○ Ability to evaluate the contribution of self and others
○ Good communication skills with adults and pupils, both written and oral.

LIST 91 Appointing TAs

When it comes to finding and interviewing TAs, it will probably be useful to discuss the process with your line manager as there may well be procedures in school that you need to follow. There will also be members of staff who are likely to be trained in recruitment protocol and will be available to offer advice.

○ Decide on a job description and the level of the job, write a person specification including qualifications, experience, type of contract and pay scale, then place the advertisement.
○ Decide on the format of the selection process – is it to be just an interview with questions, or will you ask them to take part in a lesson or complete an administrative task?
○ With the school administrator, prepare a simple pack of information to send to applicants, e.g. a map, details of the school, details of learning support or inclusion team, a job description, etc.
○ Ask a senior member of staff to shortlist with you, involve the governors and notify the candidates.
○ During the interview, check that you follow the equality and diversity processes in your school or authority.
○ Agree a successful candidate. Notify successful and unsuccessful candidates and be prepared to give feedback.

Induction

Much of this information should already be available in school but, as the SENCO you can add a pack which is relevant to SEN. The TA needs:

○ a mentor to help him/her settle in
○ to shadow an experienced TA
○ a map of the school showing classrooms, toilets, etc.
○ a copy of their job description
○ expectations in terms of dress code and names used
○ car parking details
○ a copy of the staff handbook.

The following documentation should be available for TAs (these could be put together in a handbook):

- school development plan and its aims and ethos
- staff structure – roles and responsibilities
- school routines and procedures – registers, duties for wet and dry breaks, marking systems, record-keeping, reports
- the school's behaviour management system, including rewards and sanctions
- policies on child protection, SEN, inclusion, equality and diversity and health and safety
- SEN paperwork and procedures
- relevant curriculum documents
- emergency procedures
- communication systems
- expectations of staff
- relevant information on the pupils they are involved with.

The performance management process

All TAs should be part of the school performance management process. SENCOs should make sure that their appraisal system includes the following:

❍ a self-review (sample copy in the induction materials for TAs)
❍ an observation by a more senior colleague
❍ an appraisal meeting with feedback, review of job description and previous targets and any special needs training
❍ regular repetition of the cycle.

A well-managed TA will:

❍ have a clear understanding of what is happening in their school
❍ be seen as an integral member of a team
❍ have a job description (reviewed annually) which reflects their role and responsibilities with regard to SEN
❍ be provided with internal and external training
❍ participate in policy formation
❍ be familiar with guidance regarding the support of pupils with SEN and know the school's procedures
❍ be allocated non-pupil contact time for meetings or teacher liaison time
❍ be aware of CPD opportunities
❍ be familiar with current developments in SEN
❍ be involved in the monitoring, review and target-setting process and attend review meetings
❍ maintain and promote a positive support ethos by acknowledging and celebrating pupils' strengths, successes and achievements
❍ have positive and effective relationships with pupils.

LIST 93   TAs working with teachers

If TAs are to be effective and advance the learning of pupils, it is important that the SENCO liaises with other teachers to make sure that everyone who works with them knows what to expect from their TA.

TAs should:

○ share the long- and medium-term planning
○ understand the purpose and aims of the lesson and how it fits into the curriculum
○ contribute to the planning of the lesson and understand their role
○ help prepare and collect the required resources
○ know the needs of the pupils they are supporting and any IEP targets
○ assist with classroom management and know their role
○ promote the independence of pupils
○ evaluate the pupils' learning and feedback to the teacher.

Whole-class teaching

During whole-class teaching the TA should:

- keep individuals on task by prompting and praising
- minimize distractions by dealing with individual behaviour and welfare issues
- ensure access, e.g. by simplifying or translating the teacher's language, helping a pupil formulate answers to questions or use resources, helping with signing or scribing
- sit close to pupils who need support and give them focused help, e.g. remind them of previously learned strategies, and encouraging use of correct language
- work with pupils to prepare them to answer a question the teacher has given them time to think about
- provide images, pictures and tactile, practical resources to help a pupil's understanding
- provide appropriate praise and encouragement
- support pupils with behaviour difficulties, e.g. helping them to settle and be involved, and keeping their attention directed to the task
- observe individual pupils for assessment purposes
- monitor the progress of class or individuals on behaviour targets.

Group and individual sessions

During group and individual sessions the TA should:

○ promote the independence of the pupil
○ make sure that the task will advance and promote the learning of the group or an individual
○ ensure access to the task, e.g. by scribing, signing or helping the pupil to use ICT, providing adapted resources
○ go over the teaching of an earlier session with targeted pupils to make sure it is fully understood
○ support work on teacher-planned differentiated tasks
○ ensure access to resources pupils may need in order to understand what is being taught
○ work on a structured programme
○ pre-tutor for future whole-class sessions or the plenary
○ coach behaviour or group work skills
○ supervise the class while a teacher works with a particular group.

TAs and behaviour management

As SENCO it is important to make sure that TA support for classroom management is negotiated and agreed with the class teacher before the session. TAs can help with classroom management by:

- greeting pupils on entry
- checking that they all have the correct equipment
- checking that homework is completed
- ensuring that the seating arrangements are appropriate for physical, sensory and behavioural needs
- checking that the heating, lighting and ventilation is suitable
- checking for any health and safety hazards
- using non-verbal cues to remind pupils of expected behaviours
- sitting close to pupils who may need help to stay on task
- ensuring that all pupils can access the work and that they are suitably challenged
- reminding pupils of the class rules
- if appropriate, removing a pupil for a quiet word outside the classroom
- recording homework for pupils who find it difficult
- supervising the tidying away of resources
- standing by the door to say goodbye to pupils
- checking the room is ready for the next session.

Useful Information

9

LIST 97 Software for developing and supporting literacy

Many SENCOs use ICT software to support learning in literacy. Here are some tried and tested software packages – all can be used to support structured literacy programmes or to make the curriculum more accessible.

- *Word Shark* (age range 6–16) – contains games to develop reading and spelling and reinforce word recognition. Based on the book *Alpha to Omega* (Beve Hornsby and Frula Shear) and compatible with the National Literacy Strategy.
- *Starspell* (age range 7–adult) – a look, cover, write, check-based program designed to improve spelling. Personal word lists can be created and there are a range of word lists, activities and worksheets. Includes diagnostic pupil records.
- *Nessy* (age range 5–adult) – contains 14 sections with activities to develop reading and spelling. Designed to be multi-sensory. Includes word searches, crosswords and study skills strategies.
- *First Keys to Literacy v2* – links the development of keyboard awareness to early literacy skills. Pupils can develop keyboard skills through picture-matching, letter recognition, word-building and spelling.
- *AcceleRead AcceleWrite* (age range 8–11) – a talking computer-based scheme for developing literacy skills.
- *ClozePro* (age range 5–16) – a program for producing cloze activities.

Wordbanks

- *WordBar v2* (age range 9–adult) – contains a bank of words and phrases that can be read out.
- *Clicker v5* (age range 5–adult) – can be customized for whole words, phrases and pictures. Built in speech software for listening to text. Can record your own voice.

Writing and planning

- *Co:Writer* (age range 5–adult) – a support package for developing writing, including word prediction.
- *Draft:Builder* (age range 7–adult) – a planning program that supports gathering information, planning and writing.

Talking word processing packages

- *Write: Outloud* (age range 7–adult) – contains Franklin phonetic spellchecker. Alerts pupils to word omissions, misplacements and offers correct word choices and spelling.
- *Read and Write* (age range 7–adult) – includes speech feedback, phonetic spellchecker, dictionary word prediction, text HELP toolbars.
- *Inclusive Writer* (age range 4–adult) – on-screen keyboards, word lists, picture grids, and spell checking, aided by speech and pictures.

Speech recognition software

- *IBM ViaVoice* (age range 11–adult)
- *Dragon Naturally Speaking – Preferred and Professional* (age range 11–adult)

Portable dictionaries and spellcheckers

- *Franklin Literacy Word Bank, LWB–216* (age range 5–11)
- *Franklin Speaking Homework Wiz*

LIST 98   Advice on purchasing software

ICT can be used to promote independence in learning but purchasing the equipment is usually a costly process. Support software should be planned as a whole-school approach but you may well be involved in the process of selecting and obtaining suitable material for your pupils.

○ Before you buy a program, ask for a demonstration. What looks good in a catalogue might not be suitable for pupil or staff needs.
○ Consider who will be trained to customize programs for pupils.
○ Consider who will be available to train the pupils with their new software or equipment.
○ Remember that some programs are excellent when you and the pupil are familiar with them but they can be time consuming to get to grips with in the first instance.
○ Find out where you go for support when something goes wrong.
○ Consider how accessible the computers are. At Key Stages 3 and 4 some pupils are likely to need facilities available in all lessons. Are there PCs available in all rooms, access to portable facilities or a combination of both?

LIST 99

Useful publications

There's plenty of information and publications around to help SENCOs. Try some of these as a starting point.

❍ DfES publications – Department for Education and Skills (DfES) Publications, PO Box 5050, Sherwood Park, Annesley, Nottingham NG15 ODJ. Web: www.teachernet.gov.uk/ wholeschool/SEN.

❍ SENCO Forum – http://lists.becta.org.uk/mailman/listinfo/ senco-forum

❍ *SENCO Update* – Freepost LON, 13693, 67–71 Goswell Road, London EC1V 7EP. Tel: 0207 251 9034; Web: www.optimuspub.co.uk.

❍ *Special Needs Coordinator's File* – Pfp Publishing Ltd, 67–71 Goswell Road, London EC1V 7EP. Tel: 0845 602 4337.

❍ *Special Children* – Questions Publishing, Leonard House, 321 Bradford Street, Digbeth, Birmingham B5 6ET. Tel: 0121 666 7878; Web: www.education-quest.com.

❍ *British Journal of Special Educational Needs* – NASEN, 4–5 Amber Business Village, Amber Close, Amington, Tamworth, Staffordshire B77 4RP. Tel: 01827 311500; Web: www.nasen.org.uk.

❍ *Support for Learning* – NASEN (as above).

❍ *Special!* – NASEN (as above).

Useful websites

○ ADHD
ADD Information Services – www.addis.co.uk
ADDNet UK – www.ukselfhelp.info/addnet
Attention Deficit Disorder Support Group – www.adders.org
Hyperactive Children's Support Group – www.hacsg.org.uk

○ Autism
The National Autistic Society – www.nas.org.uk

○ Cerebral palsy
Scope – www.scope.org.uk
HemiHelp – www.hemihelp.org.uk

○ Communication difficulties
ACE Centre Advisory Trust – www.ace-centre.org.uk
ACE Centre – North – www.ace-north.org.uk
Communication Matters – www.communicationmatters.org.uk

○ Down syndrome
Down's Syndrome Association – www.downs-syndrome.org.uk
Down Syndrome Education Trust – www.downsed.org

○ Dyspraxia
Dyspraxia Foundation – www.dyspraxiafoundation.org.uk

○ Epilepsy
Epilepsy Action – www.epilepsy.org.uk
The National Society for Epilepsy – www.epilepsynse.org.uk

○ Specific learning difficulties
British Dyslexia Association (BDA) – www.bda-dyslexia.org.uk
The Dyscovery Centre – www.dyscovery.org.uk
Dyslexia Institute – www.dyslexia-inst.org.uk

○ Hearing difficulties
British Association of Teachers of the Deaf (BATOD) –
www.batod.org.uk
British Deaf Association – www.learntosign.org.uk
National Deaf Children's Society (NDCS) – www.ndcs.org.uk

RNID (Royal National Institute for Deaf People) –
www.rnid.org.uk
SENSE – www.sense.org.uk

❍ Physical disabilities
Association for Spina Bifida and Hydrocephalus – www.asbah.org
Parent Project UK – www.ppuk.org

❍ Speech and language difficulties
Afasic – www.afasic.org.uk
Cued Speech Association UK – www.cuedspeech.co.uk
The Dyscovery Centre – www.dyscovery.org.uk
The Dyspraxia Foundation North London Support Group –
www.communigate.co.uk/london/dyspraxia/index.phtml
ICAN – www.ican.org.uk

❍ Visual difficulties
ClearVision Project – www.clearvisionproject.org
RNIB (Royal National Institute of the Blind) – www.rnib.org.uk
Visual Impairment Centre for Teaching and Research (VICTAR) –
www.education.bham.ac.uk/research/victar
National Blind Childrens Society – www.nbcs.org.uk
Nystagmus Network – www.nystagmusnet.org
SENSE – www.sense.org.uk

❍ Vulnerable children
Barnardo's – www.barnardos.org.uk

❍ Special needs (general)
NASEN – www.nasen.org.uk.

101 ways to say 'well done'

- You've got it made
- Super!
- You're on the right track now
- That's right!
- That's good
- You are very good at that
- That's coming along nicely
- That's very much better
- Good work!
- I'm happy to see you working like that
- Nice going
- That's the way
- You're getting better every day
- You're really working hard today
- Exactly right!
- Congratulations
- You're doing that much better today
- You did it that time!
- That's not half bad!
- Keep it up!
- You've got that down pat
- That's it!
- You did a lot of work today
- Well, look at you go!
- Keep up the good work
- You haven't missed a thing
- Now you've figured it out
- Sensational!
- That's better
- Excellent!
- Perfect!
- Way to go!
- Now you have the hang of it
- You certainly did well today
- You're doing fine

- Good thinking
- Keep on trying!
- You outdid yourself today!
- I've never seen anyone do it better
- That's the best ever
- Now you have it
- Good for you!
- I think you've got it now
- Fine!
- Good going!
- Terrific!
- You've got your brain in gear today
- Great!
- Not bad!
- That's a good boy/girl
- I like that
- Marvellous!
- That was first class work .
- Wonderful!
- Wow!
- Much better
- That's the best you have ever done
- That's it
- It's a pleasure to teach you when you work like that
- Good job
- You figured that out fast
- Go to the top of the class
- I'm very proud of you
- One more time and you'll have it
- That's great
- You're doing beautifully
- You really make my job fun
- I couldn't have done it better myself
- You're a winner now
- That's really nice
- You remembered!

- Well done
- You've just about got it
- You've just about mastered that
- That's better than ever
- Nice going
- You're really going to town
- Outstanding!
- Fantastic!
- Tremendous
- You make it look easy
- You must have been practising!
- Right on!
- Superb
- You are learning fast
- That's quite an improvement
- I knew you could do it
- Top work
- Ten out of ten!
- Nothing can stop you now
- Congratulations – you've got (number) right!
- Brilliant!
- Give yourself a pat on the back
- That kind of work makes me really happy
- Good remembering
- That's the right way to do it
- You're really improving
- You did that very well
- Now that's what I call a fine job
- Good for you
- Keep working on it, you're getting better.